GUT PUNCH

Waking up from my American Dream

GUT PUNCH

Waking up from my American Dream

By Thomas A. Koehler

© 2023 by Thomas A. Koehler

All rights reserved. This book or any portion thereof may not be reproduced or used in any manner whatsoever without the express written permission of the publisher except for the use of brief quotations in a book review.

ISBN: 9798850395650

CONTENTS

Introduction · 1

Chapter 1	The Day Our Lives Changed Forever· · · · · · · · · · · · · · ·	3
Chapter 2	Reflections—in the Beginning · · · · · · · · · · · · · · · · · ·	5
Chapter 3	Reflections of the Only Child · · · · · · · · · · · · · · · · · ·	11
Chapter 4	Reflections of One of the Original Latchkey Kids · · · · · · · · ·	15
Chapter 5	Reflections on Work Ethic and Responsibility · · · · · · · · · · ·	21
Chapter 6	Reality—October 28, 2020 ·	25
Chapter 7	Reflections on Education—1953 · · · · · · · · · · · · · · · · ·	31
Chapter 8	Reflections on a Real Job ·	39
Chapter 9	Reality—January 5, 2021· ·	43
Chapter 10	Reflections on Miller Time · · · · · · · · · · · · · · · · · · ·	47
Chapter 11	Reality—July 2021· ·	59
Chapter 12	Reflections—"California, Here I Come," July 1978 · · · · · · · · ·	65
Chapter 13	Reflections of an Undercover Man · · · · · · · · · · · · · · · ·	69
Chapter 14	Reflections on What You Wish For · · · · · · · · · · · · · · · ·	77
Chapter 15	Reflections on a Fun Work Environment · · · · · · · · · · · · ·	85
Chapter 16	Reflections on My Rocky Mountain High· · · · · · · · · · · · · ·	91
Chapter 17	Reflections on the Best and the Worst of Times· · · · · · · · · · ·	95
Chapter 18	Reflections on Change· ·	99
Chapter 19	Reflections on Romance· ·	111
Chapter 20	Reflections on Important Decisions · · · · · · · · · · · · · · · ·	115
Chapter 21	Reflections on the Happiest Day of My Life· · · · · · · · · · · · ·	119
Chapter 22	Reflecting on the Vision of Our Own Firm · · · · · · · · · · · · ·	131

Chapter 23	Reality—September 2021: The Wait Continues	135
Chapter 24	Reflections on More Changes	139
Chapter 25	Reflections on Even More Changes	143
Chapter 26	Reflections on Moving for the Tenth Time	147
Chapter 27	Reflections—What Happened to the America I Grew Up In?	159
Chapter 28	Reflections on Faith	171
Chapter 29	Reality—Living with Cancer: November 2021	179
Chapter 30	Reflections on Purpose versus Motivation	185
Chapter 31	Some Final Thoughts	191

Acknowledgments · · · · · · 195
Memories · · · · · · 197

INTRODUCTION

Try as I may, there simply is no way for me to describe the emotional reaction to a cancer diagnosis. One day you are living a normal life, involved in your normal routine, and within minutes your world is turned upside down. You long for normalcy, but from that very moment forward, the normalcy you remember will be fleeting and at times will seem unattainable. From that moment on, you are subconsciously beginning to experience the new normalcy that will be your life. If you are not careful, your thoughts can be dominated by anxiety, sadness, anger, and depression. I think it is extremely important to remain positive, but these other emotions can take over if you are not careful. I have always considered myself to be a positive person; however, I knew I would need to maintain a new level of positivity as I faced the many phases of my treatments.

One night while out to dinner with friends, after my diagnosis and treatments began, I was relating some stories from my past. My friend said, "Tom, you really should write a book. You really have had some interesting experiences." I responded by laughing and saying, "Who would want to read it?" To which she replied, "I would."

After pondering the thought of writing a book for a few days, I decided that even if no one ever read it, it might be a fun thing to do, something that might take my mind off the issues at hand. When I started writing this book, I really didn't have any audience in mind. I simply started writing to get my mind off the present. I guess it would be safe to say that my initial audience was me. Soon after I started, I began to feel the cathartic effects of the writing process. I was able to write in real time and chronicle the treatment process as it transpired—a process that took two and a half years and will continue after the book is completed; the writing process that allowed me to look back while focusing on the present with little thought on the future. I could concentrate on the now, be it cancer treatments, current events, or politics. The future is in God's hands. But I will do my part.

As I continued to immerse myself in the writing project, I began to think about the number of people going through exactly what I was. I wondered if sharing how I was dealing with cancer, death and mortality would help others. The night Carol and I learned of my diagnosis, it felt like the second time in my life I received a gut-punch-like message that I didn't deserve, the first being thirty years ago when I lost the job I absolutely loved at Miller Brewing Co. Writing this book, though, just might fulfill the goal that Carol and I set: to try to make something positive out of our current situation. In the end I hope this book and the story of how I dealt with my challenges can help others, not only cancer patients but others experiencing loss, unhappiness, and their own mortality.

CHAPTER 1

THE DAY OUR LIVES CHANGED FOREVER

The gut punch phone call I'll never forget came about 6:30 p.m. on October 22, 2020. The caller ID flashed on the TV screen, indicating that Dr. Eric Hall was calling. Carol and I were in the process of making dinner. When we were dating, staying home, and preparing dinner was our date night. We both had demanding careers, and as a result we each spent many days and nights traveling. That meant dinners out most nights. The good news for both of us was that many of those dinners were at some of the finest restaurants in America. The bad news was sometimes we tended to get spoiled.

Because of our respective demanding schedules, we really valued and treasured our time at home. Date night began a tradition we continued throughout our marriage. Thankfully, Carol is a fabulous cook, and we both really enjoy having a glass of wine and preparing dinner at home. My culinary skills are limited to the grill and assisting Chef Carol as her personal sous-chef. I never thought the chopping skills acquired while selling Cutco Cutlery part time while putting myself through school would play such a major role in my love life.

I had recently met with Dr. Hall, going over the results of my annual physical. Everything was good except that one of my blood test readings indicated I might have a gallbladder issue, for which he prescribed an ultrasound.

I answered the phone. "Hello."

"Hello, Tom Koehler? This is Dr. Hall calling. I just received your ultrasound, and after reviewing it, I have a serious concern. It appears you have sizable mass on your left kidney." As you might imagine, I stopped cold. This couldn't be. This must be a mistake. I felt great. My mind was racing, but my voice was silent. Dr. Hall filled the silence by saying he was going to call me back with an appointment to see the urologist. Luckily Carol had a relationship with a highly recommended urologist because of an ongoing kidney stone condition she had. I was on a waiting list to see him, but Dr. Hall was able to get me in the following week.

When I hung up on Dr. Hall, I informed Carol about the kidney and that he was trying to get me in to see her urologist. We stared at each other in disbelief and, without saying a word, knew that our lives were about to change significantly and would never be the same again. As we looked into each other's eyes, we toasted with our wineglasses and said, "We'll get through this together. Let's see if we can make something positive out of what will probably be the most difficult time in our lives."

As I sit here and begin to chronicle the next journey in my life, I am reminded that, unlike other journeys I have taken, this one is a little different. It may be my last. A cancer diagnosis and accepting one's mortality causes you to reevaluate your whole life. I think of the number of times I used to tell Carol, "Honey, if I die tomorrow, don't feel sorry for me or cry for me. I have had the best life I could have ever imagined." If someone had told me, back when I was a child, the things I would do and experience in my lifetime, I would never have believed it. Perhaps it is time for a look back.

CHAPTER 2

REFLECTIONS—IN THE BEGINNING

When you are periodically forced to live your life on hold, you find yourself pondering your own mortality and remembering various events from your past.

Mom and Dad's wedding picture, 1940

My earliest childhood memory dates back to sometime between when I was two and three years old. On a calendar it would correspond to somewhere between 1949 and 1950. I vaguely remember my mom bundling me up in a dark-green snowsuit with a scarf over my mouth and tying it behind my neck. I know it seems unusual for a child to remember being that young, but I recall talking to my mom and asking her how old I would have been if I remembered the green snowsuit. She was quite amazed, also, when she realized I would have been between two and half and three years old.

While I didn't realize it then, I would learn later that we piled into a 1947 Pontiac and headed to my mom and dad's place of work in Milwaukee, which was about a thirty-mile drive. Dad and Mom would drive that car for the next ten years. There were no freeways, interstate highways, or turnpikes back then. Rather, there was a two-lane road that, while it was blacktop, also had its share of potholes along the way.

THE KOEHLER CLAN, WITH GRANDPA K THIRD FROM THE LEFT, CENTER ROW

GUT PUNCH

Both Mom and Dad worked in Milwaukee. My dad worked as a boilermaker, and my mom was a beautician. My mom graduated from high school, and my dad left school after the sixth grade to go to work. Both grew up on farms. My grandfather on my dad's side—we'll call him Grandpa K—lost his wife, my dad's mother, to an accident on the farm when she was thirty-eight years old, and my dad was only eight. My dad always said it was very hard for my grandfather and he didn't think he ever got over it. My great-great-grandfather Michael homesteaded the farm in 1848. I'm unsure, but I think he eventually passed it down to my grandfather. I believe it stayed on the Koehler estate until Grandpa K sold it and retired when he was in his midforties. He bought a small parcel of land within the city limits and raised chickens.

My dad was raised by my granddad and my dad's older sister. For much of his later years, Granddad was something of a recluse. While my dad and his older sister had the run of the house, Grandpa K confined himself to his bedroom, where he spent hours and hours reading the Bible. Meanwhile, my grandfather on my mom's side, Grandpa Z, continued to work an active dairy farm well into my youth.

Dad would drop my mom and me at her place of work and pick us both up in the late afternoon and drive back to Saukville (which had a population of six hundred). Back then there was no preschool or day care. My mom was fortunate to have an employer that allowed her to bring me with her. I don't remember a time up until he retired that my dad didn't have at least two and sometimes three jobs. Before he was married, he worked as a truck driver, hauling gravel for road and local construction projects. He loved music. He was also in a band where he played drums and a German accordion by ear, with no formal training. He would play on weekends. Sometimes he would get paid, and other times it would be just for fun. He would later meet my mom at one of these events. No one could dance the polka better than my dad. Later he would buy his own truck to supplement his factory income.

One of the most traumatic events I recall as a child was when my dad was hospitalized for a disease called bronchiectasis. It is a lung disease in which the lungs' airways become damaged, usually the result of infection or a medical condition like pneumonia. While I'm sure things are different today, back in 1953 it was life threatening. Back then, young children were not allowed in the hospital for visiting hours. I remember my mom coming home from the hospital and crying for hours. She tried to explain to me that my dad might not be coming home again. I would cry with her, not understanding much of anything other than that she was sad and I thought I should be crying too.

He was being cared for in the Saint Alphonsus Hospital in Port Washington, Wisconsin. Later, when I was older, I would learn that they brought in a lung specialist from Milwaukee to operate on my dad. They removed about one-third of his lung. Prior to the surgery, he was given last rights by the Catholic priest that happened to be visiting other patients that day. Although we were Lutheran, my dad had a special relationship with the priest, as he had volunteered his time and equipment to help build a shrine on the property of the local Catholic church. Later, after his recovery, my dad would talk about the fact that he thought the priest played as an important role in his recovery as did the surgeon. At the time we were told that he was one of the first patients to survive the surgery.

I remember when he was on the road to recovery and was able to get up and move around, my mom took me to the hospital. While I was still not allowed to visit him in his room, there was a balcony where they brought him in a wheelchair. From the first floor lobby, I was able to look up and see him wave to me and Mom. We were all crying, and I remember Mom explaining to me that it was OK to cry because these were happy tears.

Soon after that he returned home for the long recovery. I remember a blur of people coming to visit, bringing food, flowers, and liquor. His friends would joke about how the liquor was for the celebration they would have when he was fully recovered. I don't recall whether they ever had the celebration specifically for the recovery, but I do recall many parties that would follow throughout my childhood. All of them would involve him playing his accordion. In later years, they would also include his son, me, playing an accordion alongside him.

When I was six or seven years old, my dad was laid off from his boiler-maker job and relied on his trucking business to maintain the family income. Mom always supplemented the family income and continued working part time into her seventies. Dad never forgot the important role that the insurance benefits played in our lives because of his lung surgery. In his mind we would have been ruined financially if he had not had the extremely good benefits from his factory job. He said while he could make good money with his trucking business, he was afraid we couldn't survive another catastrophic health issue. He said he would settle for less pay if the benefits were good.

Me with Dad's first truck and my first dog, Schpoozel

Ultimately, he would get another full-time factory job in Port Washington, Wisconsin, working at Simplicity Manufacturing, which made lawn and garden equipment. While working full time at the factory, he would expand the trucking business to a full-blown excavating business with a bulldozer and other heavy equipment. He would come home from the factory job at 4:00 p.m., eat a quick supper, and get in his truck and go to the excavating site until 10:00 p.m. There were many days I didn't see him at all. He would be gone before I got up for school and would not return until after I was in bed. He did it all by himself, with my mom doing the bookkeeping.

Later, when I was in high school and had a driver's license, I worked for him, driving truck and learning about the other heavy equipment we used in the business. As I look back, I can honestly say he was the hardest-working man I ever knew. And throughout his life, I don't remember him ever complaining about anything. I read somewhere since my cancer diagnosis that the journey from diagnosis to acceptance makes the individual more appreciative. While I always appreciated my parents and the many sacrifices they made for me, it wasn't until I began writing down some of these things about my dad that I truly appreciated what an unbelievably strong and hardworking individual he was.

CHAPTER 3

REFLECTIONS OF THE ONLY CHILD

In the last one hundred years, researchers have conducted numerous studies on only children to determine whether the stereotype of the spoiled only child is true. Interestingly, results have been mixed. While it's true that only children may receive more attention from their parents, this doesn't always lead to self-centeredness or selfishness. We all know someone who is selfish and has siblings. If anything, only children may have stronger bonds with their parents and are extremely independent. I believe this to be true.

My first experience with the term "only child" occurred at a family gathering with other cousins and young children. For some reason I have always been alert to my surroundings and still am today. In this case I was listening to the adult chatter in the background when I heard my name mentioned in conjunction with a negative connotation regarding the term "only child." "Of course, he is so well behaved—he's an only child," one of my aunts or one of the older adults said. The tone of her voice translated to me as "he is spoiled." I don't think I was more than five or six years old at the time, but my reaction to that incident stayed with me my whole life. I never wanted to feel like I had been given something I didn't deserve but rather cherished the feeling of reward for working hard and receiving the benefits. I hated the thought that I received special treatment simply because I was an only child.

My dad had a horse when he was a teenager and into his twenties. I recall that when I turned seven, he and Mom decided I was old enough to begin to have some responsibilities other than helping with the dishes. So, for my seventh birthday, they bought me Major, a fifteen-hand-high pinto quarter horse. My mom always said Dad really wanted another horse but just used me as an excuse.

TEACHING MY DOG DAISEY TO RIDE

The problem was that we lived on one and a half acres of property in the country with no barn and no fence. We had a one-and-one-half-inch steel rod about three feet in length that would need to be pounded into the ground and attached to a long leather strap. When Major ate all the grass in the area covered by the strap, we would have to pull the rod out of the ground and move it to a new area so he could get fresh grass. The strap was about thirty feet in length, so the grazing area was a circle with a sixty-foot diameter, and the rod needed to be moved almost daily. Moving required pulling the rod out of the ground and then pounding it into the ground in the new spot. I learned how to swing a sledgehammer at a young age.

GUT PUNCH

My Best Friend Major

Eventually, my dad and grandfather built a small corral. My dad found a timekeeper shack that was being discarded with the completion of the construction project he had worked on. He and Granddad converted it into a small barn. In the summer months, we could run a garden hose from the house to the barn, but in the winter, I had to carry buckets of water to fill the trough. Sometimes this would require boiling-hot water to thaw any frost or ice that developed in the trough. Trust me when I say that taking care of a horse was far more work and a lot more difficult than caring for a goldfish or hamster.

Major would bring me much happiness and satisfaction. Because I was an only child, he was my companion. He was a good listener. When I shared some of my childhood frustrations and feelings, I never had to worry about feeling stupid or, even worse, having him tattle on me to Mom and Dad.

During that period, I joined the local 4-H club. It was a club where young children would be able to follow and expand their various interests with adult supervision and mentoring. My project one year was Major. We were judged on grooming and various gate disciplines, including walking, trotting, and galloping, while our horse was handled by only a halter and a leather lead. One of my proudest childhood moments occurred when my mom and dad, Major, and I were lined up at attention before the competition while a local vocalist sang the national anthem. While we all stood with our hands over our hearts listening to the anthem, I began to get a lump in my throat and tears in my eyes. I tugged on my dad's shirt and asked him why I was crying. He looked down at me, smiling, and said, "Don't worry, Tommy, it's a good thing. Someday when you're a little older you will understand." When the song ended and the applause followed, my tears vanished as fast as they had appeared. The entrants were ready for the competition. I still choke up today when the national anthem is played.

Major and I won second place in our division and were awarded a red ribbon, which I proudly clung to until we returned home later that day. It was displayed in the Koehler family home for years to come, a visual reminder that my hard work and discipline paid off and had nothing to do with being an only child.

CHAPTER 4

REFLECTIONS OF ONE OF THE ORIGINAL LATCHKEY KIDS

Rex and Daisy, also known as Schnapps

While my mom always tried to organize her days so she would be home from work when I got home from school, periodically something would come up. I would occupy most of my free time taking care of Major. My childhood home was located on the Milwaukee River, about one and a half miles north of the nearest town, Saukville, primarily farm country, with a few individual houses along the way. We had two neighbors, each with one child my age, and there was a childless couple about a mile away.

While I would occasionally play together with the children, my interests were different. My horse—and later rescue dogs, Daisy and Rex, and a boat—would occupy my free time. I would go horseback riding while Daisy followed along and go fishing in the river behind our house. Most of the time I would fish from shore. In the early years, I would catch bass and occasionally a northern pike or some crayfish. At the time, the river was unpolluted, provided much enjoyment, and occupied much of my free time. In the winter, when it froze, I would ice-skate after school until dark. Occasionally we would have ice-skating parties. There were never enough kids to play hockey, but we would still attempt to go through the motions with three or four kids.

By midsummer the river levels would be relatively low. There was one area behind the farmer's pasture where it was deep enough to swim. We didn't have water wings, noodles, or plastic rafts. We had old inner tubes from Dad's trucks and cars. One summer I taught myself to swim, much to my mom's distress. Neither she nor my dad could swim, so naturally they were very concerned about my safety. In most places behind our house, the river was too shallow, so they had nothing to worry about. Like most kids, I always had to push the envelope. I would take one of the inner tubes and float down the river to the swimming hole, where I would slip the inner tube under my arms and pretend to swim. Moving my arms and kicking my feet, I would practice the basics. This worked fine until I slipped out of the tube one day and started to sink to the bottom. Frantically slapping my arms on the water and kicking my feet, I managed to reach a shallow part of the river where I was able to stand up. Slowly perfecting my strokes and kicks, I began to swim.

Although never a strong swimmer, and certainly not strong enough to swim competitively, I became comfortable in the water. Eventually we would tie a rope to a tree limb along the river so I could swing out over the water and splash down, cannonball-style. Daisy would jump in the water and try to race to the spot where I would land. While I initially gave my mother a heart attack when she watched me swing out over the water, she eventually grew accustomed to the sight and became at ease with it.

GUT PUNCH

We had an old wooden rowboat that leaked and was way too big for the depth of the water in the river behind our house. Daisy and I would go for boat rides and constantly run aground or get stuck on the rocks. Even Daisy got frustrated with me constantly having to get out of the boat and lift it off the rocks. Sitting in his plastic mesh reclining lawn chair, smoking his cigar, and watching Daisy and me struggling with the rowboat, my dad thought he'd solved the problem.

First boat

Second boat

Realizing we could not remove all the rocks in the river, he decided that the problem was the deep-V design of the hull of the rowboat. His solution was to build a flat-bottomed scow-design boat just for the river behind our house. By the time Daisy and I returned to shore, he described how we would build a flat-bottomed boat with two two-by-fourteen-inch planks as the sides of the boat and aluminum sheeting for the bottom. In addition, he would put a paddle wheel on the stern and power it with a four-horsepower Briggs & Stratton lawn mower engine. He recruited our neighbor, who also considered himself a self-taught engineer, to help with the construction.

Miraculously, six weeks later we were ready for the christening. We launched the boat and started the lawn mower engine, and away I went, only to discover a slight design problem. The rudders were too small to turn the boat. With no reverse and the ability only to make a slight turn, we obviously had a serious navigation hiccup. But not to worry; the two engineers already had a solution: increase the size of the rudders on the stern and add a large rudder on the bow.

We relaunched the following weekend, and the motorized scow provided Daisy and me hours and hours of enjoyment. I guess the boating bug bit me when I was eight or nine years old and stayed with me throughout my life. I bought my second boat, *Wild Thing*, when I was a junior in high school and was bitten by the waterskiing bug. By this time, I had a car, and my dad was able to help me get a job in the factory where he worked for the summer. While Mom and Dad took a rare one-week vacation that summer, I was invited by one of my dad's friends to Random Lake, Wisconsin, where he would have his ski boat. He planned on being there for the weekend with his family. He promised that if I came to the lake, he would teach me to water-ski.

Well, I went to the lake, and he taught me to ski. I was addicted after the first ten minutes, and I was able to get up on my first try. As I drove home, I knew I had to buy a boat. I couldn't sponge off my dad's friend, and I wanted to be able to introduce some of my friends to the sport. It was a Sunday, and on the way home, I stopped to buy a Sunday paper. Armed with the ads for boats for sale, I spent the evening going through the classified ads. By the time my parents came home that weekend, my almost-new

GUT PUNCH

boat was parked in the driveway. I know my dad wasn't thrilled with the fact that I would be speeding around the lake water-skiing, but he did help me install a permanent hitch on my car. I knew he wouldn't criticize me because I used my own money earned from the summer job, he had helped me to procure.

CHAPTER 5

REFLECTIONS ON WORK ETHIC AND RESPONSIBILITY

GRANDMA AND GRANDPA Z WITH COUSINS

Despite being an only child, I never felt alone, although most of my activities were done solo. Between my chores, taking care of Major, my fun time with Daisy and Rex, boating and fishing on the river behind our house, and pheasant hunting in fall, any free time I might have had to get in trouble was pretty much used up. I always looked forward to summer vacations.

Most years summer vacation would begin around mid-May. The timing would coincide with my summer vacation on Grandpa's farm. I would usually stay with Grandpa and Grandma for a couple of weeks at a time throughout the summer. It was a great opportunity to spend time with my two cousins who lived on the farm as well.

My first visit of each year coincided with haymaking season. Grandpa owned a dairy farm with several head of dairy cows. More than half the acreage was planted with alfalfa to provide feed for the cows during the winter. The rest of the acreage was planted with corn and oats. There were two haymaking seasons, spring/summer and late summer/early fall. Today, even all these years later, I can still close my eyes and smell the fresh alfalfa. It was the sign that always told me spring had arrived.

My grandfather recruited me to help during the hay season by telling me I could have some of the hay for Major if I helped him. My mom and dad were paying twenty-five to fifty cents per bale of hay, and it was my first opportunity to help contribute to Major's maintenance.

I learned a lot from my first summer vacation with Grandpa. A day on the farm started around 4:00 a.m. when the weather was good. We would first have to round up the cows for milking. Once the milking was completed, we would all pile into the kitchen for a big breakfast Grandma would prepare. The "making hay" part would then begin sometime after breakfast, usually around 8:00 a.m. Grandpa would hook the bailer to the tractor. After that he would hook a large wagon behind the bailer, forming a three-piece train of equipment. Once equipment was prepared, off we would go to the hayfield. The field would have been prepared days before by rolling recently cut hay into neat rows.

Grandpa would then drive the tractor, pulling the bailer so the incoming chute would line up with the row of hay. As he drove down the row, the hay would go into the bailer and come out the end in a neatly packed rectangle-shaped bale, held together by two pieces of twine. My job was to pick up the bale and neatly stack the bales on the wagon, starting at the very back of the wagon and working forward, stacking them as high we could stack them. Each bale weighed about fifty pounds. We would return to the barn to unload and go back out for another wagonload.

Lunch was usually a big noontime meal, which is why our evening meal was light and referred to as supper. Grandma would make everything from cold-cut sandwiches to mashed potatoes and pork roast. My favorite was fried chicken. It didn't come from Kentucky Fried, but rather fresh from the farm that morning.

My grandfather had about one hundred eighty acres. The planted crops included hay, oats, and corn. The hay crop of about eighty acres was planted and harvested twice per year, once in spring and once again in late summer or early fall. The hay crop had to be enough to feed the dairy cows all winter long.

I'm sure that when my parents bought Major for me, there were those who once again brought the "only child" term into the conversation. If getting up at 4:00 a.m. and working until sunset was their idea of spoiling the child, what would they recommend as an alternate activity?

The summer vacations and my grandfather's farm prepared me for my first paid summer job. There was a dairy farm about a mile from where we lived. My mom would periodically buy fresh eggs and milk. Mom told the farmer about my summer vacations and haymaking experience at Grandpa's farm. Half-serious and half in jest, the farmer, whose name was Peter, told Mom that since I was now an experienced twelve-year-old, if I was looking for a job, I should contact him. When my mom told me, I got on my bike and rode off to my first job interview. Two hours later I returned and proudly announced I was now a hired farmhand specializing in baling hay and making one dollar and fifty cents per hour. And so I took my first step on my lifetime journey of working for a living.

I would work for Peter on the farm for the next several summers. In addition, I supplemented my farmwork by helping my dad with his excavating business. While I had no hourly wage working for my dad when I was younger, my allowance was eventually replaced by an hourly wage as I got older.

Good habits started at an early age. Every Friday evening, we would go to the bank. I would stand in line at the teller's window to make our deposits. My mom helped me open my own savings account and insisted that I make a weekly deposit from my weekly jobs. The old saying "save for a rainy day" became meaningful in my life at an early age. As I approached the age of sixteen, my motivation heightened. Being of legal driving age would mean I needed more money for a car.

Grandmother offered to help me with the purchase price of the car if I promised to pay her back and cover maintenance and insurance. With the car came my second paying job. This time it came from my dad speaking to one of the county commissioners and learning they were going to be building a golf course about five or six miles from our house. No skills were required. I qualified as a stone picker. The land that would eventually become a county golf course needed to be cleared and excavated. Once again, I would ride my bike to the site; I had a whole summer to wait before I turned sixteen and could obtain my driver's license.

As the fairways were excavated, they needed to be prepared for planting. That preparation included freeing them of stones and other obstacles. This required someone driving a tractor pulling a stone boat, followed by someone picking up the stones that surfaced and throwing them into the stone boat. I can't begin to estimate the number of steps or miles I covered that summer. I literally walked behind that tractor picking up rocks five days a week, eight hours per day, from June through August. Needless to say, I really cherished overcast days and a chance to get out of the sun. I am proud to say that of all the young boys my age that volunteered for the job, I was the only one that lasted the whole summer. Perhaps this is why I never developed an interest in becoming a golfer. Now I have more important things on my mind.

CHAPTER 6

REALITY—OCTOBER 28, 2020

The morning of Oct 28, 2020, Carol and I visited Dr. Rodin, our urologist, for the first time. He had reviewed the ultrasound and confirmed the mass on my left kidney. He told us that in situations like this, they assume the mass is cancer until proved otherwise, but before we proceeded with addressing the kidney issue, he would order additional tests to determine if there were any other areas of concern. He ordered CT scans of my chest, abdomen, and brain as well as bone scans. He advised that once the results were reviewed, we would discuss next steps.

Getting the tests completed consumed the next several weeks, and by November 9 we were back in Dr. Rodin's office. Our hope was that we would be discussing next steps in addressing the kidney cancer. Our hopes were dashed, however, when Dr. Rodin told us that the various CT scans also revealed a small nodule in my right lung. So, before we could get too far along on treating the kidney, we would need to biopsy the lung and then begin to consider the course of treatment. He told us that the kidney would most likely have to be removed, and while he used to do the surgeries, he now recommended that we go to either the University of Miami or the Moffitt Cancer Center in Tampa. He also suggested we get a local oncologist. Over the years we had known several individuals who had very high praise for Moffitt, so we selected Moffitt and the professionals there to take our next steps. With Dr. Rodin's referral, we were scheduled for a virtual consultation with Dr. Alice Yu, the kidney surgeon, for November

25, 2020. Everything I had ever heard about cancer treatment indicated that time was of the essence.

Our emotions were improving with the belief that we were making progress on treatment. Unfortunately, our hopes were again dashed when the lung needle biopsy turned out to be inconclusive. By this time, our oncologist, Dr. Yeckes-Rodin, who happens to be married to Dr. Rodin, our urologist, got involved and recommended that Dr. Jacques-Pierre Fontaine, a thoracic surgeon from Moffitt, perform a surgical biopsy or simply remove the nodule. After consultation with Dr. Fontaine, lung surgery was scheduled for mid-January. Dr. Fontaine, one of the foremost thoracic surgeons in the country, called the house—another example of the degree of professionalism and personal care found at Moffitt.

The next critical date was the virtual consultation with the kidney surgeon. Depending on the pathology report for the lung, the initial treatment would include immune therapy to see if the tumor could be shrunk, therefore possibly eliminating the need for surgery.

Thanksgiving Day was the next day, and our celebration was subdued. We avoided most of our friends' inquiries regarding holiday plans because we didn't want to spoil their holiday season with my medical problems.

Carol's mom, Ursula, was scheduled to come for the annual holiday visit in the beginning of December, so we were unable to avoid any discussion. It was extremely frustrating that no treatment could begin until the pathology on the lung was completed. The frustration was compounded by the constant threat of COVID-19. My number one priority—and Carol's—was to avoid contact with the public as well as close friends. When it came to our friends, we just didn't want to talk about it until there was something definite to discuss.

Our first challenge was determining how to tell Carol's mom. We didn't want to tell her not to visit for the holidays, yet we knew that her flight and possible exposure to COVID was a risk we would have to take. Carol's mom has one of the strongest religious faiths I have ever known. At eighty-seven she went to mass every day. She strongly believes that her health is in God's hands, and back in December of 2020, wearing a mask was not a high priority for her. We told her about my diagnosis prior to her flight in hopes that it would provide an additional incentive for the mask habit. Needless to say, the Christmas season at the Koehler house was subdued. We tried hard to stay positive and put on happy faces.

We were doing fine until the morning of Christmas Eve. It was difficult accept that there were no symptoms. The morning of Christmas Eve, everything changed. That morning I had a significant amount of blood in my urine. We immediately placed a call to Dr. Yu. She returned our call almost immediately. We would learn over time that that was the Moffitt culture. As we talked, she advised me that she felt the kidney should be removed immediately.

Her first available time was January 4. This would require two trips to Tampa, the first for preop and the second for the actual operation. Our schedule immediately went into high gear. First, would Ursula stay or return to Chicago before my surgery? We would need to kennel Savannah, our dog. We would need to arrange for lodging near the hospital. Ever since the "gut punch" phone call in October, I'd felt like my life had been put on hold. I was existing with the sole purpose of survival and that survival depending solely on the actions of others. The more we interacted with people at Moffitt, the more our confidence grew. They were among the most caring and professional people with whom I have ever dealt. One of the first examples of that was when Dr. Yu was scheduling the kidney surgery. I advised her that I also had lung surgery scheduled for January 15 and asked whether that would conflict. Her response was simply, "We'll handle all the rescheduling on our end. You just worry about staying healthy and COVID-free and getting here for your surgery."

Ultimately, Ursula would return to Chicago on January 1. Savannah would have reservations in the Charleston Suite at the Palm City Animal Clinic, which came with a CCTV camera, allowing us to check on her from our cell phone in the hospital. We would ultimately stay at the Hilton Embassy Suites, about fifteen minutes from the hospital. The most difficult part of Dr. Yu's request would turn out to be getting to the hospital for my surgery safely. The week before the scheduled surgery, we made our first trip to Moffitt in North Tampa for my preop consultation. I was tested for COVID, had blood drawn, had an EKG, and received my COVID vaccination. During the consultation, we learned that the actual surgery would take about five hours. Depending on how I responded, I would be required to stay one or two nights and then released. I would recuperate for the remainder of the month and then come back for my lung surgery.

Sunday, the day before my scheduled surgery, while traveling from our home in Palm City, we experienced a tire blowout on Interstate 4 in Tampa. That experience was probably more life threatening than the surgery itself. We were forced to call 911, which in turn sent a highway safety ranger to assist in changing the tire—if you can imagine trying to change a tire with your car positioned against a concrete barrier on the right while cars traveling at seventy miles per hour plus passed us on the left. As the ranger and I knelt to work on the front left tire, we could feel the wind currents on our backs from the passing cars.

After surviving the tire blowout on the way to the hospital on Sunday, we arrived at the hospital at 5:30 a.m. for preop. Shortly after arrival we were called into the staging area. Patients scheduled for surgery are assigned a small bed on wheels in an area separated by curtains. There is no room for modesty. You remove all your clothes and put on a gown, which is open in the back, and wait. Shortly after you model your ass-exposing gown, several members of the team—the surgeon, anesthesiologist, and a group of nurses—once again interview you. Then you wait some more.

I never questioned that my kidney surgery would be successful. This same operation a few years before had been considered high risk. I knew a few people who'd had the surgery in the last several years, and all were living perfectly normal lives. Nonetheless, as Carol and I learned as we waited, you always think that there is a possibility something could go wrong. We occupied ourselves with small talk until they rolled me away sometime after 8:00 a.m. I looked forward to the well-deserved sleep I would soon be experiencing once the anesthesia was administered.

The operating room was brightly lit and filled with the surgical team. I was quickly transferred to the operating table, positioned with my left side up so the surgeon could have access to my left kidney, and my face was covered with an oxygen mask. I was told to take a few deep breaths, and that is the last I remember until I woke up in my room about five hours later, surrounded by Carol, my surgeon, and several nurses inquiring about my pain levels. All I remember is saying that I just wanted to go back to sleep and that my stomach felt like I had done about five hundred sit-ups. My pain was controlled with a combination of Tylenol and oxycodone.

    The next few hours are a blur, but I do remember the nurses helping me walk by early evening. Overall, the recovery in the hospital is a fog in my memory. It's hard to believe that I could have been released by 4:00 p.m. the next day, but I was. Now the focus would be recovery, so I could be ready for my lung surgery in four weeks. More time to think. Think about cancer. Think about death. Think about the life I so enjoyed.

CHAPTER 7

REFLECTIONS ON EDUCATION—1953

A light breeze comes through the one-room schoolhouse. All the windows had been opened earlier in the morning with the arrival of Mrs. Whittier, my teacher. In 1953 there was no air-conditioning. As a matter of fact, there was no indoor plumbing and no running water. If you wanted a drink of water, you used the hand pump outside the front door of the schoolhouse. There was a tin cup tied to the pump, and below it was a bucket to catch anything that spilled from the cup because you usually had to pump the handle a couple of times to get to the colder water and water that was not left in the pump from the previous user. We all drank from the same cup, and to my knowledge no one got sick.

The room accommodated forty to fifty children ages six through fourteen. The room was laid out with eight rows of approximately six individual lift-top desks in each row, facing the blackboard. Yes, a real honest-to-goodness blackboard. Not a green board but a blackboard. Each of the eight rows was dedicated to one grade, one through eight, with first grade in the first row, the second grade in the second row, and on through the eighth grade.[1]

---

1 *History & Reflections from Wisconsin* by Jerry Apps.

THE COVER OF JERRY APPS'S BOOK CAPTURES THE ESSENCE OF MY FIRST SCHOOLHOUSE

    The teacher would start by standing at the blackboard in front of the first-grade children and teaching their lesson for that day. After about forty-five minutes, she would move to the second graders in the second row and again administer their lessons. This routine would continue throughout the day, finishing with the eighth graders. We would have a twenty-minute recess in the morning and midafternoon and a forty-five-minute lunch break. In the spring and fall, we were permitted to extend our lunch break and the recess time for outdoor activities like softball and kickball. In southeastern Wisconsin, below-zero temperatures were not uncommon. The children walked to and from school. By the time October and November rolled around, outdoor activity in Wisconsin was limited.

For the first couple of years, we would all walk to school. For me, it was about a mile and a half. One girl actually rode a donkey from her nearby farm. There were no days off for rain or snow. We would simply wear our raincoats and boots in the rain or bundle up for snow and sleet in the winter.

Bathroom facilities were known as outhouses. There were two, one for the boys and one for the girls. There were holes cut into boards to form seats. There was an attempt to have adequate supplies of toilet paper in each of the outhouses; I recall that old Sears catalogs were always available as backup. Once in the classroom, the children would have to ask permission from the teacher to use the bathroom. In the winter this meant that once you received permission, you had to go to the outer entry, where we kept our coats and boots, get completely dressed in your winter clothes, and trudge to the outhouse, which was located about seventy-five yards from the schoolhouse, far enough away keep the raunchy odors out of the schoolhouse.

Heat for the schoolhouse was provided by a coal furnace located in the basement. There were no custodians in those days, so making sure there was adequate coal in the furnace to provide heat for the day fell on the shoulders of the upperclassmen (twelve- and thirteen-year-olds), who stoked the furnace. As I look back at those days, it seems we were forced to grow up sooner than the kids today. We were given responsibility early in our lives, and we were expected to accept that responsibility.

Our school was located in the country and surrounded by farmland. I can still remember the first days of spring. The windows would be open. The breezes would carry the scents of the day. In early spring the wind could be filled with the not-so-pleasant odors of farmers spreading manure on the adjacent farmland in preparation for the spring planting. Then in late spring, those scents would be replaced by the pleasant aroma of freshly cut alfalfa. As I think back to that time, I can still smell those pleasant scents today, a reminder of my youth.

While my recollection of those early education years is sketchy, I remember liking school. I have a real appreciation for my mom, who, regardless of how busy she was, insisted on starting my education at an early age at home. I can remember the pride I felt when I was five and was the only kid who knew the Lord's Prayer on my first day of Sunday school. That same pride would be felt in first grade, where I would once again know the alphabet and even some addition, subtraction, and multiplication. Because of the way the schoolroom was laid out, I could hear what the teacher was teaching the second graders. Because of my mom, I had a head start on my first-grade lessons, so I would listen to the second-grade lessons while my fellow first graders were learning the alphabet. By the time I reached the sixth grade, the community school system consolidated and built a new schoolhouse. The new school had three classrooms and a gymnasium. Most importantly it had running water and indoor plumbing. I would no longer be in a classroom with all eight grades, but I would still be in a room with fifth- through eighth-grade children.

Throughout grade school and the first two years of high school, I was a pretty good student. I made the honor roll my freshman and sophomore years. The wheels came off about the same time I got my driver's license and discovered a social life.

Higher education was more of an afterthought than a priority until the second semester of my senior year in high school. Since my dad had not graduated from high school, I originally thought I would do just fine since I

GUT PUNCH

planned to graduate. But after the total of my labor market experience—my summertime jobs, working on farms, picking rocks on the golf course, and several construction jobs, one of which required me to work about 150 feet in the air—I decided to rethink the whole college decision. As a result of my lack of foresight, I only now came to realize that the entry process would require both the satisfactory completion of the SAT test and an acceptance. I was totally unprepared.

Since my parents lacked the funds to send me away to college, my choices were limited. I was able to complete the SATs and be accepted by the University of Wisconsin at the Milwaukee campus. I would commute every day from my parents' home about thirty miles away.

To say that I was totally unprepared for the college experience would be a total understatement. In 1967 the Vietnam War was in full swing. I needed to be enrolled in an accredited college before my eighteenth birthday to be eligible for the draft deferment. So, the clock was ticking. Until the second semester of my senior year of high school, I had spent no time thinking about college, much less a major. So before my graduation came along, I had to successfully pass the SATs, choose a major, and pick my class schedule for the fall semester of my first year in college. By now I am sure you can see where this is headed. By the end of the second semester, I had flunked out of UWM.

Knowing my university experience was soon coming to an end, I decided I needed to pursue some type of continuing education. One day a good friend of mine and I were walking down the street in Port Washington, Wisconsin, when we noticed a former Port High graduate driving through town with his brand-new 1966 Pontiac GTO. I remember thinking it was one of the most beautiful cars I had ever seen: a powder blue convertible with a white leather interior. I asked my friend if he knew what the former classmate did to be able to afford that car. He told me that he believed the classmate had gone to a private business school in Milwaukee and upon graduation went to work for Mobil. That did it. The next week I drove to Milwaukee and enrolled in Spencerian Business College and decided on a business administration degree. As I said, I had been totally unprepared for the university experience I encountered at UWM, with the large class sizes, the lecture auditoriums, and the excessive (to my mind) number of elective classes required. I had been taking astronomy, geology, and philosophy and couldn't understand why. At business school, I was taking all classes that pertained to my career choice. Accounting, public speaking, and marketing just made more sense to me. All the classes contributed to the skills I would need in my business career.

Now that I was reenrolled in school, three obstacles remained between me and my new Pontiac GTO. First, I would need to graduate in four years, and second, I would have to find a part-time job. And since I'd lost my deferment when I flunked out of UWM, my education could be interrupted by a two-year hitch in the army. The draft was eliminated in 1973, but the transition to a volunteer military was ushered in by a selective service lottery. On December 1, 1969, all the days of the year were figuratively thrown in a hat, and individual birthdays were drawn. If your birthday was drawn early, you most likely would be drafted. If your birthday was drawn later, you would probably not be drafted. My birthday was drawn in the 352nd position, virtually guaranteeing me a pass on the draft.

While I still wasn't in a position to buy my new GTO, I was one step closer. Now I had to find a job. Because most students at Spencerian were working their way through school with limited parental contributions, most relied on part-time jobs. The class schedules allowed for either all-morning or all-afternoon classes, leaving either mornings or afternoons for jobs. I was able to find several part-time jobs during this time. One was working for the company that was building the freeway system in Milwaukee. My job was to be a timekeeper for all the employees and to take injured workers to the hospital. It was a great job, paid extremely well, but one requirement was that I had to be on the jobsite at five in the morning.

Somewhere along the line, I had learned that you don't give up a good job unless you have something better lined up. Spencerian had an employment office set up to help students find part-time jobs to help pay for their education. I would check the information board regularly for available jobs and new listings. One day I came across an ad for a sales position that allowed you to choose your own hours. At first blush it looked to be an improvement over getting up every morning at 4:00 a.m. I was the only person to show up for the interview. The company was Cutco Cutlery, a subsidiary of Wear-Ever Cookware of pots-and-pans fame, all owned by the Alcoa aluminum company.

I was very gullible. Little did I know that they hired anyone with red blood in their veins and a pulse. The presentation was very persuasive. I would not only make 25 percent on what I sold, I would also receive another 5 percent on sales from anyone I recruited. It was a typical pyramid scheme, but I was too naive to realize it. It was the finest cutlery in the world with a forever guarantee—not a lifetime guarantee but a forever guarantee. Our customers were single working girls between the ages of eighteen and thirty. Nothing wrong with that. That, plus the fact that there were two new Corvettes in the parking lots owned by two of the salesmen I met that night, cinched my recruitment.

I'll never forget the expression on my dad's face when I proudly announced I had a sales position with Alcoa. My first sales pitch was to my mom, when I asked to borrow the money for my sample kit. My dad almost choked when he asked how much all this cutlery cost and I told him *only* $350 (in 1967 dollars). I remembered the sales manager said to always say "*only*" before any reference to price. I think the closer was when I explained that if the job didn't work out, at least my mom would have a great set of cutlery that came with a *forever* guarantee, and if the job worked out, they could take credit and some pride in every set of cutlery I sold that contributed toward my tuition. It was like they were paying for my tuition with every sale I made. What a salesman!

Cutco set up a sales quota and promised that if you achieved it, they would cover each semester's tuition. While some people made out very well, the majority of the new sales reps would sell to their family and friends and then give up. My goal was, at the very minimum, to make enough to pay back my mom and dad, just to make sure I never heard the words "I told you so."

In the long run, a new 1969 competition-orange 427 Corvette Stingray with side pipes eventually became my powder blue GTO, and Cutco paid for all my tuition, in that I reached the sales quotas for every semester I was selling Cutco. I averaged about $10,000 per year (in 1967 dollars) in commission selling knives door to door to single working girls—and an endless supply of girls' phone numbers. I would later take a cut in pay when I took my first job after graduation. Life was good! And I never heard the words "I told you so." To this day I'm still partial to powder blue GTOs because one provided me with more motivation than I ever anticipated.

They say life is a game of choices, and I can now look back and say that my decision to work for Cutco was one of those choices, even though my dad thought I was nuts. When you are working on straight commission, knocking on doors, if you didn't sell, you didn't eat. I learned the value of discipline and focus, and working for Cutco acted as an ongoing course in developing people skills and communication skills. Along with communication skills, I learned listening skills, but most importantly I learned the importance of a positive attitude. When the customer gave their final *no*, you had to pull yourself up by your bootstraps and knock on that next door—but sometimes maybe not.

I recall a time I was training a recruit. It was important that they had a good experience and would not be afraid of the noes, because if they were successful, I would make 5 percent off what they sold. In this case there was a woman working in her backyard while the recruit and I were walking past. I engaged her in conversation, trying to get her to listen to my sales pitch. She ultimately became a little angry with us and told us to move on. Because I didn't want my recruit to have a bad experience, we walked around to the front of her house, and I rang the doorbell. My recruit looked at me like I was nuts. When the woman came to the door, I smiled and said, "Hi, ma'am, I sure hope you're not as grouchy as the woman in the backyard and would listen to my sales pitch for the world's greatest cutlery. You don't have to buy anything, and if you just listen, I get credit toward my tuition." She broke into a big smile and finally said, "OK, but I don't plan on buying anything." She ended up buying a little over a hundred dollars' worth. I made twenty-five bucks and saved my recruit from a bad experience. The old making lemonade out of lemons was alive and well.

It was a great job while I was in school, but I knew that upon graduation I would need to take a new direction. The big question was, what direction would I take?

CHAPTER 8

REFLECTIONS ON A REAL JOB

Someone once said that failure is part of life, and with every failure you get closer to success. Looking back, my failure at the university certainly put me on track for my future business career. In the spring leading up to my graduation, several of us piled into my car and drove to the Palmer House in Chicago for the job fair that was being held that week. We spent the day researching possible future employers and interviewing with recruiters. It was a hectic day but certainly worth the experience. Of the four of us, I was the only person to receive a legitimate job offer that day. Ortho Pharmaceutical offered me a position in Ohio, selling birth control pills to doctors. The recruiter was very open and honest with me and said that my experience selling door to door was all he needed to offer me the job. I turned it down because I didn't want to relocate to Ohio and ultimately took a job with Panasonic selling industrial closed-circuit TV products.

I will never forget the day we received a call from the Milwaukee Bucks' front office. They were inquiring about the use of our products for their training department. I was able to set up a demonstration for later in the week with the coaching staff and some of the executives. Needless to say, I was a little nervous. At the conclusion of the presentation, I asked for the order and got it. Only one requirement. They would need someone to travel with the team so their staff could be trained on the use of the TV and tape-recording equipment. Are you kidding me? I would have paid them for the opportunity.

Naturally I made the ultimate sacrifice and volunteered to travel with them for their next game. It was an exhibition game played against the Phoenix Suns. Unfortunately, the Bucks lost, but before boarding the bus, I purchased several programs with the intent of getting some autographs from the team. Since I was traveling with the team, I naturally felt like I was part of it. One of the Bucks stars was their newly acquired center, Lew Alcindor. At the time he was the talk of the NBA at seven foot one; he would later change his name to Kareem Abdul-Jabbar. When I approached him and asked for his autograph, he basically laughed at me and told me he didn't give autographs. As we deboarded the bus, he was walking behind me when I passed a garbage can. I got his attention one more time to tell him how much I appreciated his autograph in a not-so-polite manner, while throwing all the programs I had purchased in the garbage. I can say that that experience affected my opinion of professional athletes to this day.

It was a good job but offered very little future. I worked there for over a year. One of my roommates, who was having some difficulty finding a suitable job, came home and announced that he'd gotten a job with the Miller Brewing Company and would be relocating to Sioux Falls, South Dakota. We all gave him a rough time, telling him, "No one drinks Miller. Are you nuts? There are only pheasants in South Dakota." He told us that the tobacco giant Philip Morris had just purchased a part of Miller and had an option for the rest in the future.

This was in the early seventies, and unemployment was high. For the next year, my friend would tell us how great it was working for Miller. He encouraged me on several occasions to apply. He went so far as to set up an interview for me, which I forgot about and didn't show up for. He had been in the job for about one year when he came home to visit and told us that he had been promoted. He said, "Tom, you really need to apply. I'll set up another interview for you, but this time, show up. It really reflects badly on me if you don't. Besides, it's a great job. They pay us for doing what we like to do most: drink beer! Plus, you have access to an endless supply of cigarette samples." That was the clincher. Kind of like selling Cutco to single working girls and getting the added benefit of never being short of phone numbers.

GUT PUNCH

In 1972 Miller Brewing Company was the thirteenth-largest brewery in the United States. Milwaukee breweries like Pabst and Schlitz both outsold Miller, and Pabst was the most popular brand in the area. Miller had a reputation for tasting skunky and usually did. I think it would be safe to say that up until July 1972, I probably had never drunk Miller beer. Although my parents and I were big beer drinkers, Miller was not our beer of choice.

I went to the interview, and halfway through the interview, I knew I really wanted this job. I was hired to replace my roommate and was sent to Sioux Falls, South Dakota. The guy who didn't want to go to Ohio was now on his way to South Dakota. Once again, my dad gave me a vote of confidence when in jest he said, "Were you the only one that showed up for the job again? That worked out pretty good for you. Maybe this will too."

So in July 1972 I embarked on a journey that would last the next twenty-five years and provide me with some of the most satisfying and rewarding moments anyone could expect from their career. My official title to start was area manager. Area managers were assigned a geographic area and were responsible for all Miller business in that area. The overall objective was to increase sales in the area and improve the business practices of the distributors within the area. The company did not have a sophisticated training department in those days. Training simply consisted of riding along with an experienced area manager and observing what they did, hopefully picking up the good habits and avoiding the bad. After about a month, I was called into my manager's office, where he presented me with a briefcase full of files and told me to go to South Dakota and be an area manager. He told me he would be out to see me in the next few weeks to see how I was doing.

CHAPTER 9

REALITY—JANUARY 5, 2021

Now back to the present. Reluctantly we left the hospital late afternoon on January 5 and made our way to the hotel where we would spend the night before heading back to Palm City in the morning. The doctors were sympathetic to our desire to stay one more evening but explained that with COVID and other infections that were usually prevalent in a hospital, they thought that it was better for me to leave. While I was enjoying my anesthetic-induced sleep followed by the enjoyable fog brought on by my painkilling drugs, Carol spent her time getting the car repaired. So often we concentrate on the individual with cancer and forget about the loved ones who care for them and may be left behind.

Carol was busy finding a Lexus dealer near the hospital. The nurses had been in communication with Carol by phone throughout the surgery. When it was appropriate, she was contacted and advised that I was OK, out of surgery, and in recovery. After she saw the whites of my eyes, she would then have to prepare for my discharge and our trip back home. First, though, we needed to repair our car.

Luckily, she located a Lexus dealer nearby, and after she explained our circumstances, they were able to schedule her for necessary repairs. Our plan was to stay in the hotel near the hospital the first night and if everything remained stable, head home midday Saturday. In a strange way, Carol's activity was probably a blessing in that she would be so busy she would not have time to ponder my condition and would maybe worry a little less.

We made it home around 3:00 p.m., grateful to be in familiar surroundings and begin the recovery process in preparation for my next surgery in four weeks. Looking back, I can't imagine taking this journey alone, yet so many people have to do just that. Thank God for the support groups and others that help people who have no loved ones in their life.

The weeks after my kidney surgery are still a blur. I lost about fifteen pounds, and my activity was restricted for about two weeks. The associated pain was being managed by the combination of Tylenol and oxy. I was frightened by the long-term effects of the oxy. The doctor prescribed about a month's supply, but out of fear of addiction, I wanted to get off the oxy ASAP. Each day I would try to extend the time between doses, and after about two weeks I was off the oxy completely and relied on just Tylenol.

The inactivity of recuperation made the emotional effects of the cancer diagnosis even worse. I didn't want to die. I felt too good to die. I wasn't as worried about myself as I was Carol. It gets to the point where it is all you think about. The doctors were confident that they had removed the cancer, which included the left kidney and the associated lymph nodes; however, the pending lung surgery was still a lingering concern.

My recovery went smoothly but slowly. I was able to get back into a routine. By January 20 we were back at Moffitt for the postop exam. They were able to schedule the postop for my kidney and the preop for my lung surgery for the same day, saving us an extra trip to Tampa. They also scheduled my second COVID vaccination. Once again, we experienced the professionalism and high level of medical technology at Moffitt. Dr. Yu was happy with the progress of my recovery, and Dr. Fontaine was confident I would be ready for my lung surgery in two weeks. By late afternoon we were back on the road, heading home to Palm City.

Carol and I began to think we were making progress. One major surgery completed successfully, and one to go. Of the two surgeries, the kidney was considered the more complicated and therefore more worrisome. We didn't want to jinx ourselves, but we were slowly beginning to be a little more optimistic.

In three short weeks, we were back at Moffitt in preparation for my scheduled lung surgery. By now I was a pro. On Thursday, February 11,

GUT PUNCH

Carol and I once again found ourselves in the operating staging area, this time less the stress associated with the blown-out tire on Interstate 4. Once again by midafternoon I was coming out of anesthesia and seeing the smiling face of my beautiful wife. Once again, I was scheduled to spend the night in the hospital and to be released the next morning.

This time, however, there was a complication, and by Friday I was unable to clear my bladder. The doctor on call at the hospital refused to release me. She said this reaction to the anesthesia was not uncommon, but policy dictated release protocol. By Saturday morning I was still unable to satisfactorily clear my bladder, and the doctor prescribed a catheter be inserted that would need to be removed by my doctor back in Palm City on Monday morning. By late Saturday afternoon, the catheter was inserted, and a bag attached to my leg, and we were on our way back to the hotel.

By noon on Super Bowl Sunday, we were back on the road to Palm City. On the road home, Carol left a message at my doctor's office regarding the removal of the catheter the next day. By 8:00 a.m. Monday, my urologist was calling to tell me that if we could be there by 9:00 a.m. he could remove the catheter, or I would need to go to the hospital because he was leaving by noon. Needless to say we were there by 9:00 a.m. Once again, I would be on those wonderful drugs, but once again, I would force myself to stop them before all the pain subsided. The risk of addiction far outweighed their short-term advantage.

Carol and I began to think that there was light at the end of the tunnel. All traces of the kidney cancer were gone. Now, the doctors were waiting for the pathology report regarding the lung surgery. They were quite confident that it, too, was kidney cancer that had metastasized to the lung. They felt that because it had been caught so early and all removed, I would be cancer-free, and I would be able to return to somewhat normal existence, understanding that I had only one kidney.

Two weeks after the surgery, we were back for the postop and my second COVID vaccine. Once again, my hopes to a return to normal existence were dashed when the doctor advised us that the pathology report indicated the cancer was not kidney but rather melanoma. That meant that the melanoma cancer cell was in my system and would most likely reappear in the future.

I have always been plagued with skin cancer problems, and for the last ten years had seen a dermatologist every two months. I had various types of skin cancer removed on many of my visits. About three years ago, I had a melanoma removed from my armpit, as well as three lymph nodes. In retrospect we think that is where it came from.

We were advised that there were two courses of action. One, do nothing and follow up with periodic C-scans, hoping to find it when it appeared. The second was to begin a new form of treatment of what was called immune therapy with a recently approved drug called Keytruda. Chemo was no longer prescribed for melanoma, as it had been found to be inefficient. Like chemo, Keytruda required intravenous transfusion. These half-hour transfusions would be done locally every three weeks for at least a year. I was scheduled for my first treatment for March 1. Always the optimist, I considered this a good omen because March 1 was my mom's birthday. I guessed I would have more time for reflection.

CHAPTER 10

REFLECTIONS ON MILLER TIME

My first official duty as an area manager was to fly to my new territory and find my company car. My manager told me it was a green 1972 Ford Torino. He gave me the keys and said it was parked somewhere in the parking lot of Joe Foss Field, the airport in Sioux Falls. He said he should have made a note of the license plate number but had forgotten. "Don't worry, Tom, the airport in Sioux Falls isn't that big. You will find it." And so my journey would continue.

Finding the car turned out to be the easy part. No problem. The problem was a dead battery from sitting idle in the parking lot all those months. Once I was able to get assistance, I was ready for the second priority on my new journey: finding a place to live. While I'd left home when I was eighteen, I had always had roommates. This time would be different. The company was flexible with my relocation and work schedule while relocating. I set up temporary housing in the downtown Holiday Inn in Sioux Falls. I delayed house hunting for a few weeks to get to know my local Miller distributor and get the lay of the land. The distributor was Carlsen Distributing, owned by Harry and Vera Carlsen. Vera ran the office, and Harry managed the warehouse, truck fleet, and sales. They had a son, Mark, who had recently graduated from college and helped with the sales.

Harry and Vera were a typical hardworking Midwest couple. As I'd hoped, they were a tremendous help to me in getting relocated. Thanks to Harry and Vera, I was able to find an apartment in a new complex with indoor and outdoor swimming pools and a sauna. For the unsophisticated country boy from Saukville, Wisconsin, this was a big deal! It would be several weeks before I was able to move in. This would give me a little time to organize my move.

My territory encompassed distributors doing business in four states, South Dakota, Minnesota, Iowa, and Nebraska, totaling fifteen distributors in all. The eastern border of the area extended from Alexandria south to Rochester along I-90. I organized my first business trip to encompass my distributors in Minnesota so I would end the week in Worthington and be able to return to Milwaukee for the weekend. There I would rent a U-Haul to move what few belongings I had and return to my new apartment to set up housekeeping. I needed to buy some furniture and begin my new career in Sioux Falls, South Dakota.

When all the tasks were complete, I remember the feeling of pride and independence. While it wasn't much, the new apartment was mine, and I would build from here.

For the next three years, I would learn the beer business from the bottom up. The first thing I learned was that the beer business is a people business. To be successful you needed to be able to handle all types of personality, big egos or humble folks. All the distributors were family owned, and back in 1972, these distributors sold several brands of beer, and Miller beer was usually not their largest seller. Harry and Vera also sold Grain Belt beer. The brand sold more than Miller, and up until I got to Sioux Falls, I had never heard of it.

The second thing I learned was that the corporate culture was in flux. Much of the old Miller culture was characterized by the "good old boys" attitude, but the new culture, as demonstrated by the new Philip Morris–appointed president, John Murphy, was results oriented and dynamic.

In my opinion there were four executives responsible for turning a sleepy little brewery located in the Miller Valley in Milwaukee, Wisconsin, into a major force in the industry. In addition to John Murphy, there were Lauren Williams, a thirty-five-year-old VP of marketing; Ed Frantel, VP of sales; and L. J. Goldstein, who later replaced Ed Frantel when he was promoted to president and CEO of 7UP, another Philip Morris subsidiary. These individuals were smart, competent, and visionary. They were tireless workers without an ego, no matter how successful they became. As a result, leadership by example was evident in most of the senior management positions. Where it wasn't, those managers were soon replaced with those who would demonstrate it.

I was very fortunate to be exposed to such qualified and effective managers early in my career. I was young enough and inexperienced enough to not have developed a lot of bad habits. Working with such great role models was very instrumental in developing my own management style. I could pick from things I observed that were effective and discard those traits that I observed that didn't work or I disliked. Lead by example, think through the issues, and be firm but fair in dealing with others.

The new culture rewarded creativity and a "let's get it done" attitude. It remained that way for the next twenty years, but the culture would eventually fall victim to the corporate politics brought in by senior management people recruited from other companies and other industries.

For the next three years, I was on a fast track, not sure where it would end. I was promoted to larger territory thirteen months after I got to Sioux Falls. I covered the northern tier of Illinois, including the Chicago suburbs, and the southern tier of Wisconsin. Eleven months later I was again promoted to another new territory. This one was in Budweiser's backyard in Saint Louis, Missouri. In those three years, I learned the beer business from the bottom up. For the most part, the Miller distributor network in the mid-1970s was hardworking but somewhat unsophisticated. While the "good old boys" culture was alive and well in the sales organization, this would change if the new, more aggressive marketing-oriented culture eventually permeated the distributor network. It became obvious that for Miller to be successful, the distributor network would have to go through a major overhaul.

In trying to develop a good working relationship, I tried to maximize the time I spent working with and for the distributor, trying to improve their business. My strategy was simple: if I was making the distributor's business better, he would be more likely to help me. I discovered early that if people like you they are more likely to work with you than if you come across like someone who thinks they are important just because they work for the brewery.

It didn't take long to develop friendships as well as healthy working relationships. And neither did it take long for distributors to share their observations of past Miller area managers. I soon learned that they fell into two categories. Some were arrogant and egocentric because they worked for the brewery. Others were more down to earth and sincerely tried to help. You can guess which style worked best.

From that my management style evolved. I would lead by example. I would not be afraid to get my hands dirty. I would try to sell people, not tell. I developed a reputation for being firm but fair. These personality traits I would carry throughout my career. To learn the business from the bottom up, I developed a routine where I regularly rode the trucks and helped the driver salesmen rather than criticize what they were doing. I would ride with the salesmen, sales managers, and owners. One of the salesmen once told me that until I arrived on the scene, his owner never left his office. I always felt that to be successful, you needed to know the market. If you knew the market, and perhaps knew it better than your competition, you could not help but be successful.

Implementing the Miller market plan was the priority of the field-sales force. By the mid-1970s sales were rising so fast that we had to allocate beer shipments to the distributors. The sales turnaround was the result of three significant marketing strategies. First, there had been a taste problem. That was followed by a quality control problem. Multiple focus groups would eventually produce the taste profile that management was looking for. Once that was achieved, the problem was that if not properly rotated in the warehouse and on the shelf, the beer developed a skunky taste. Philip Morris management authorized the pickup and destruction of all old beer in the market and reimbursed the distributor for its cost, with only one caveat: from then on, the distributor would be responsible for keeping fresh beer in the market. Failure to do so would jeopardize their contract with the Miller Brewing Company. This was the first tangible evidence of the change of culture.

Innovative marketing and creativity produced two innovations early on. The first was in packaging, when the seven-ounce pony bottle was introduced. We knew that the flavor was on target, so the more we could get people to sample the product, the better sales became. The introduction of the seven-ounce pony bottle accomplished exactly that. People were now drinking fresh Miller High Life for the first time in years, and they liked it.

The second innovation was the introduction of a low-calorie beer. Shortly after buying the Miller Brewing Company, Philip Morris, much to the surprise of industry watchers, bought the Meister Brau brewery in Chicago. At the time many of those same industry watchers rolled their eyes, sure that the tobacco company really didn't know what it was doing. Under the radar was the little-known fact that Meister Brau owned the trademark "Meister Brau Lite." Philip Morris bought the company to get control of the trademark. A few months later, Lite Beer from Miller—"everything you always wanted in a beer and less"—was introduced to a test market. This introduction was supported by what would become one of the most successful advertising campaigns in the beer industry, and many believe it to be one of the most successful campaigns in consumer products. Miller Lite was a tremendous success, and overall beer sales for Miller would continue to skyrocket, putting more pressure on production. As a result, Miller embarked on an aggressive brewery-building process over the next several years. Going from one brewery in Milwaukee, we eventually built breweries in Fort Worth, Texas; Irwindale, California; Albany, Georgia; Eden, North Carolina; and Trenton, New Jersey. (The brewery in Trenton ultimately never opened.) Miller Brewing Company grew from the seventh-largest brewery in 1972 to the second largest, selling over thirty-seven million barrels in 1980. The management team at Miller was delivering. Both sales and production were running like a top.

Improving distributor performance and professionalism, the third element of the strategy, was slowly beginning to take place. The VP of sales, Ed Frantel, described it by comparing it to a large cruise ship changing courses. In the beer business, your brands are only as strong as your distributor network. You can have the best advertising in the world, but if the distributors can't get the product on the shelf and keep it there, your brand will fail. It soon became obvious that the field-sales organization would have to identify those distributors that could be improved and get them up to speed, terminate the ones that were unwilling to make the commitment to improve, and consolidate smaller distributors into larger, stronger distributors where possible. Our strategy was simple: build the distributor network into the strongest, most professional sales and delivery system in the industry. Accomplish that, and sales would follow.

My first exposure to distributor termination was during my assignment to Saint Louis, Missouri. My territory was selected as one of the test markets for Lite because of some of the unique characteristics of the market: this was Budweiser's backyard, and there was a heavy concentration of African American residents in Saint Louis, Missouri, and East Saint Louis, Illinois. The African American market skewed to stronger beers like malt liquor, and we were curious whether there would be any sales at all and whether the advertising, which was sports oriented, would attract black drinkers.

From the beginning the distributor in East Saint Louis was reluctant to order the beer. We had invested heavily in the market, with advertising and various point-of-sale material, and here we had a distributor that didn't think it would sell and didn't want to order the beer. While the distributor was an independent businessman and had the right to refuse, it was highly unusual that they would go against the corporate directives. The owner of the distributorship was white, with a rather big ego, in a 100 percent black community. He eventually ordered a minimum quantity and was making a halfhearted effort to secure distribution.

Our frustration reached the breaking point when I arrived at the warehouse one morning to find he had installed the truck decals for Lite upside down on his trucks. While they were his trucks, we had paid for the decals and their installation. His agreement required he implement our marketing plans to the best of his abilities. When I reported the incident to my senior management, the termination process was initiated. Over the next several months, we would assign his territory to the adjacent distributors.

Distributor terminations back in the 1970s were infrequent. With our efforts to upgrade the distributor network, the number of terminations would increase. With terminations came lawsuits and sometimes violence. I didn't learn until years later that one of the distributors had hired security people to stake out my house and keep an eye on me until the termination process was completed.

GUT PUNCH

I recall another incident that at the time was concerning—some might say even frightening—and made an impression on me that lasted a lifetime. It occurred at a time when I had recently been transferred to a new territory. As was my custom, the first couple of months in a new area was a "get to know the territory" period. I also used to refer to it as the honeymoon phase. It was a learning period in which I evaluated the distributor and kept my observations to myself until I learned enough about territory to discuss it intelligently with the distributor and his management team.

In this instance, I consistently had difficulty getting an appointment to see the distributor principal. Several months went by. I was able to work with all the distributors in the area with the exception of this one. I was even able to work the market with several of his employees, yet every time I had an appointment to see him, it would be canceled or I would be pawned off on one of his employees. After consulting with my management on the proper course of action, we decided it was time to address the issue from a position of strength. After one of the handoffs, I simply addressed his secretary and advised her to tell her boss that if I did not hear from him by the end of the week, I would be contacting our legal department to initiate termination procedures. I advised her that it was just not possible to continue a business relationship where the owner was unavailable.

Two days went by, and I received a phone call from the principal. He advised me that he would meet me at a local restaurant for lunch the next day and explain his absence. When I arrived for lunch, he had reserved a table in the rear of the restaurant, situated in a darker and more secluded part of the establishment. In addition to the principal, his general manager was also in attendance. Since I had already met the GM, I felt I had the beginning of business relationship with him, but the mood could be described as somber at best.

We began with the traditional business handshake and sat down. Since they were already drinking Miller Lite, they invited me to join them, which I accepted. The principal began by apologizing for his absence and the difficulty I was having in establishing contact. He said he fully understood the frustration I must have felt but was confident that when I heard the story, I would understand completely. He explained that over the previous six months the mob (his words) associated with a neighboring large city across the state line had been attempting to infiltrate some of the businesses in his community. They were trying to put people on the payroll of legitimate business in return for protection. Otherwise, as it was explained to him, he might experience unnecessary expenses associated with his facility, trucks, and other aspects of his business, including personal harm to employees and himself. He advised me that he essentially told the people involved what they could do with their threat. For his personal safety, he then limited his availability and visibility, which is why I was having so much trouble meeting with him.

When I heard the story, while I was in shock and was having some difficulty believing it, I said that I appreciated that he had taken the time to explain the circumstances and that we would do what we had to do to work around the problem until it was resolved. He said the authorities were involved and he was hopeful that things would return to normal soon.

After forty-plus years, I admit my memory of some of the details is a little sketchy, but sometime after our lunch, one morning's news included a report that someone had been murdered in the parking lot of a popular restaurant and the suspect had been apprehended before he got out of the parking lot, as there was a police car in the lot at the time. For the purpose of the story, let's call the suspect Alex. Several weeks later, the principal and I were having lunch when a man came over to our table to say hi to the principal. The principal then introduced me, saying, "This is Tom, our area manager for the Miller Brewing Company. Tom, this is Alex." I learned in the discussion that followed that Alex had recently been released on bail. I don't know the connection, and I really don't want to know.

By 1975 I was promoted to my first management position: regional sales manager. I would now have area managers reporting to me. I was the youngest regional sales manager ever promoted, so the pressure was on. For the next two years I was responsible for the sales in Illinois, Iowa, and Missouri, as well as a portion of Wisconsin. I would now have direct reports and begin working on my leadership and motivational skills.

In 1977 I was promoted to the position of regional manager in the Capitol region. In this position I had budgetary responsibilities as well as sales and general supervisory responsibilities over ancillary staff positions. I relocated for the fifth time in five years to Washington, DC. With the move to DC, I would complete the purchase and sale of four houses in five years as well.

My assignment on Jan 5, 1977, was a result of major personnel changes at the senior level. To further diversify the company through acquisition, Philip Morris was in an acquisition phase. In an effort to shield assets from potential tobacco litigation, they acquired General Foods, Oscar Mayer, Tombstone Pizza, and 7UP in a series of acquisitions. As a result, our VP of sales was promoted to president of 7UP, opening positions in Miller sales organization and creating upward mobility for many of us.

Up until now, my experience was confined to the Midwest. It was my understanding at the time that Miller beer was far more popular on the East Coast and that my job would be a little easier. My territory was now made up of the states of Maryland, Virginia, West Virginia, and North Carolina, as well as part of South Carolina and DC. In general, the distributor network was more professional and significantly more effective. It was pleasant not having to worry about terminations and being able to concentrate on making what was already good better. Because of Miller's spectacular growth, there was a significant amount of upward mobility and opportunity for individual advancement.

As a regional manager, I was now responsible for hiring and firing as well. In an effort to improve distributor performance, we also had to upgrade our field-sales representatives, which resulted in early retirements, promotions, and employee terminations. From the time I was in charge of the Capitol region, I think we probably turned over 80 percent of the field-sales personnel. I was able to build my own team, and many would experience the same upward mobility that I had.

Being young, single, and in the beer business in Washington, DC, was a pretty good combination. One experience I will always remember occurred on the first Saint Patrick's Day celebration in DC. I had told my regional sales manager to rent a limo and that he and I would hit some of the most popular drinking establishments in the district. Our first stop was the McDonald's drive-through so we could have a good base in our stomachs for a day of beer drinking. We had advised the distributor that we would be out evaluating his distribution efforts and placement of point-of-sales merchandising in the market. The distributor had no idea whether there would be two or twenty people in the market checking up on him, and we obviously didn't tell him it was only the two of us.

As the day went on, the bars became busier. The celebration began to intensify as the offices began closing and the occupants were ready to party. By early evening we began to collect some hangers-on. Some would travel to the next bar, where we would gain new hangers-on and leave the old ones. When the ladies asked us what we did for a living, we told them that we worked for a limo service and that the boss let us use the limo once a year, for Saint Pat's Day.

As the night went on, we had a slight fender bender traveling from one bar to the next. One of the ladies that joined us said she was an insurance agent. We'll call her Jane. Jane decided to help the limo driver ensure the proper paperwork was complete. It was of little concern to me because that was one of the reasons we hadn't driven ourselves. Soon we were on our way, and Jane said she had helped to be sure no laws were broken. A little strange, I thought, but to each their own. As the night progressed, there appeared to be a mutual attraction between Jane and me developing. I didn't believe she was an insurance salesperson any more than she believed I worked washing limos. Since I knew that she wouldn't see me again unless I told her what I did for a living, I decided to confess—on the condition she told me what she did. You can imagine my surprise when she took my hand and placed it in her handbag, where she directed my hand to what was unquestionably the butt of a revolver. When she withdrew my hand from the handbag, she also showed me credentials that indicated she was a Secret Service agent. She had been assigned to be part of Rosalynn Carter's protection detail earlier in the day. Much to my dismay, we were never able to meet for dinner or a date because of her schedule or mine, and I eventually just gave up.

I had been in the Capitol region about a year and a half when I received a phone call from the new VP of sales. He advised me he would be coming to my regional office for a meeting with me the following week and I should clear my calendar. This was a big deal. I had met him only once in person, when he appointed me to the Capitol region. Business was good, so I was curious about the purpose of the meeting. He said he would explain when he saw me. Before his scheduled arrival, we all worked double time to be sure our office was neat and organized. Back in those days, there were ashtrays on every desk; after all, we were owned by Philip Morris. We went through all our distributor files to be sure everything was up do date.

In my five short years, I had never had the VP of sales visit a regional office and had no idea what to expect. When he arrived, after greeting the staff, we walked into my office, and he closed the door. My office was set up with two visitors' chairs opposite the desk and a sofa along the opposite wall. He chose the sofa, which left one of the two guest chairs for me to pull to the sofa. I certainly wasn't going to sit at my desk when the "main man" was sitting across the room on the sofa.

He began by explaining that they were reorganizing the field-sales department, adding another director to the three existing divisions. They were promoting the regional manager in the southern Pacific region to the newly created director's position and were looking to fill that vacated position. I was finally able to take a deep breath. He was here to discuss one of my guys for the open position in Los Angeles. Jumping into the discussion, I said, "That's great. I have just the guy to fill that position." I launched into how well prepared my guy was for the assignment. I never considered he was here to talk to me about the position. I had only been there a little over a year, and it would be a lateral promotion for me.

When I finished expounding my candidate's qualifications, he simply held up his hand and said, "We've already made our decision, and the replacement we want is you." He said, "I realize it's a lateral move for you, but we need you to go out to Los Angeles and build the market. Los Angeles is huge, and we aren't selling anything now. The potential is phenomenal. We have distributor-morale problems; our sales force personnel are not performing, and we think you are the guy that can fix it." When I told him I still hadn't unpacked some of the boxes from my last move, he simply smiled and said, "Good; then you won't have so many to pack this time."

The following week I was on my way to Los Angeles, with no idea of what to expect.

CHAPTER 11

REALITY—JULY 2021

As I came to understand the reality that my cancer was more serious and would require more than successfully recovering from the two surgeries, I began to accept that the journey and time for reflection would be considerably longer than we originally hoped for. One of the first things you come to realize is the vast amount of support that exists within your circle of friends. After the successful completion of the two surgeries, Carol and I began to share with our friends what had been happening in our lives in recent months. As our friends and relatives began to learn of our situation, we were overwhelmed with the prayers of well-being and hopeful thoughts.

We soon learned people were reluctant to ask, not because they didn't care but because they didn't want to intrude on our privacy or seem nosy. Because of my faith in God, I have not been afraid of death. My fears are for Carol. She is the love of my life, and without her my life would be meaningless. For the last twenty-five years our life together has been like living a dream. To say my love life was disappointing up until I met Carol would certainly be an understatement. While I am not going to go back and relive my failed relationships and analyze the reasons for failure, I'll simply say there was enough blame to go around. Speaking solely for myself, youth, immaturity, and being too focused on my career would take a good share of the blame for two failed marriages.

Carol and I first met skiing in Vail, Colorado. I had purchased a condo in Beaver Creek with a good friend and high school classmate. We both loved skiing and Vail. While my friend lived in Vail, his business took him back to Nashville, and I was living in Milwaukee. We both worked ridiculous schedules, so we wanted to have the condo for our own personal skiing and, when not in use, rent it for additional income. It was managed by the Hyatt Regency in Beaver Creek and turned out to be a very profitable investment at the time.

My administrative assistant, who was a very attractive African American woman, was part of a group of women calling themselves the Ski Amigas, of which Carol was a member. They used to plan ski trips to Vail between Christmas and New Year's every year. I also planned ski trips during the holiday and met Carol when she was skiing with the group.

Six years later, now living in Chicago, I was having dinner across the street from my apartment at Topo Gigio. I was a regular at this establishment when I was in town, which was only about one or two days a week. At the time I was working for a private equity firm called Hicks, Muse, Tate & Furst. The firm was the group that successfully consolidated A&W, 7UP, and Dr. Pepper into a stand-alone company called DPSU, of Plano, Texas, which was later sold to Cadbury Schweppes. In those days I spent most of my time flying around the country with the management company, which was hired to do the same type of consolidation in the beer industry involving the second-tier breweries Schlitz, Pabst, and Stroh.

The bartender at Topo's and I had become friends, and that night a young, attractive woman was sitting at the other end of the bar telling jokes. She had us all in stitches, especially when she was apologizing to the priest sitting next to her for telling a dirty joke. I was about to ask the bartender to introduce us when she asked the bartender if he had seen "Kuch" lately. I recalled that Kuch was Carol's nickname, but what were the chances that it was the same girl? So instead of asking the bartender for the introduction, I asked about Kuch. He said she was an attractive, perky blonde and that he understood she was in Colorado for the weekend, looking for a condo, because she was a big skiing enthusiast.

While I remembered Carol to be a very attractive and interesting woman at the time we met in Vail skiing, I admit that the overriding reason to contact her was that she might have an interest in buying a one-third interest in our condo. My partner and I had discussed possibly selling an interest to free up some money for other investments. I called my former administrative assistant the next day to see if she still had Kuch's phone number. She did, and now so did I. I called Carol the next day, and we set up a dinner date for the following Friday evening. We went to a high-end Italian seafood restaurant called Mare's.

As we got to know each other, it became obvious to me why I was attracted to her. She was real, confident, and intelligent without being full of herself. I could tell why she was successful in her career. But more importantly, I could tell she was just a good person. Sometime between our salads and entrées, we briefly reviewed the pictures of my condo and miscellaneous real estate brochures. At one point she looked at me and said, "I'm pretty sure I can't afford your condo, but if you would like to take me there someday, I would love to go." By that time, I knew that was exactly what I wanted as well.

We continued to get know one another before we moved on to Pops for Champagne for an after-dinner drink at the piano bar. Pops was a popular late-night piano bar featuring champagne and cigars. I became convinced that I wanted to spend more time with Carol to explore our relationship when she bought me a very expensive cigar to enjoy at Pops. That was the clincher.

Her "really good person" trait is what constantly displays itself as the cancer journey continues, and I can't imagine facing this journey with anyone else. We were able to schedule my immune therapy treatment here in Stuart, Florida, eliminating the potential round trips to Tampa every three weeks. Carol accompanied me to the first treatment the morning of March 1. After checking in with the receptionist, we took our seats in the waiting area.

One of the first things you learn when you are diagnosed with cancer is how many people are also going through similar challenges. The waiting room was packed with all kinds of people of different ages, races, and sexes. As I sat in the waiting area, I looked around and saw people just like me in various stages of treatment—people with skull coverings or just wrapped in blankets while they waited for the next treatment. It goes without saying that it was very depressing to observe these people and wonder whether this was what my future looked like, and if so, what kind of life would that be? Living the dream seemed like ages ago.

While we waited, we were surprised to see one of our neighbors arrive for treatment as well. He was unaware of my condition, as was I of his. Three weeks later I would receive a phone call from him wishing me well for my second treatment. Little did I know that in just a little over a year from then, I would be going to his funeral.

The sensitivity and caring qualities of people supporting those recently diagnosed is amazing. Here we really didn't know each other that well, but he remembered I was scheduled for treatments every three weeks and called me prior to my next treatment. I'm embarrassed to say I didn't remember his next treatment, nor did I make the call.

Now waiting for my seventh treatment, it is difficult to describe the emotional ups and downs. Six months since my surgeries, I have had two CT scans, both of which were clear and showed no indication that my cancer had returned. I have always been a person that lives for the future. Now I can only hope that the future CT scan will be clear as well. You need to learn to live from CT scan to CT scan. If I'm lucky, eventually the frequency of scans will be reduced from every three months to six months and beyond. I'm scheduled to continue to get the treatment for a year. Based on every three weeks, that is seventeen treatments in total. So I'm not even halfway through the process.

It's now been about six months since the diagnosis. Try as I may, I cannot remember what my life was like prior to the cancer. What did I think about when I got up in the morning? Did Carol and I have something fun planned for the day or weekend? Now the thought of cancer occupies most of the waking hours. It's so hard to think positively when you know that cancer is in your body and could show itself at any time. It's especially hard when you know that your well-being depends to a great deal on your ability to stay positive.

The treatments themselves are pretty much nonevents. I receive the drug Keytruda intravenously, much like chemo. It takes about an hour. By the time you consider the drawing of blood for the testing and the consultation with the oncologist, it's usually about one and a half hours. While side effects differ from patient to patient, I have been extremely fortunate: headaches, minimal muscle soreness, and brief bouts of nausea. My biggest concern is emotional and making sure I'm doing everything I can to leave Carol prepared for life without me. I'm just not sure how I can do that other than be sure all our financial affairs are in order.

Orienting Carol is proving to be challenging. I try to put myself in her position, and I imagine my life without her, and nothing seems to matter. The only thing left at that time in my life with meaning would be our dog, Savannah. I would cling to those things we shared. I would never want her to spend the rest of her life alone, yet I know that she could never be replaced by someone else. Nor would it be fair to that person. A person whom I would constantly compare to Carol? These are the thoughts you live with.

When you love someone with everything in your soul, it is impossible to think of the void without being emotional. Crying on a daily basis becomes the norm. Laughter takes a bit of a different role as well. Things that might cause us to bicker during the normal day became laughable. I think in some ways we tend to laugh more at things that otherwise might upset us. After a cancer diagnosis, you truly do value each day you're given.

I am writing these thoughts on the Fourth of July. As the background noise of the TV plays various patriotic songs, I find myself tearing up, just like I did all those years ago when I was standing with my horse, Major, and Mom and Dad at the county fair. I can't help but recall all the different places Carol and I celebrated the Fourth. We truly have been blessed—from the mountains of Vail to the seaside beaches of the Bahamas, the Florida Keys, east and west coasts of Florida, and the Gulf of Mexico on our own boat. Yet this year I looked forward to celebrating again with Carol. The location was unimportant; it only mattered that we were together. And we were. We were able to spend the Fourth of July with our dear friends Jim and Nancy and had a great barbecue at Carol's tennis club.

I started the holiday week with my seventh immune therapy treatment. At my prior treatment, I had discussed with Dr. Yeckes the fact that because of COVID and my surgeries, I had missed my midyear physical. I inquired whether, since they were drawing blood from me every three weeks, they could also draw what I would need for my other tests. She said they could.

I then checked with my GP and cardiologist to determine what blood tests they would need and came prepared with a list of additional tests that needed to be run.

On July 9, at about 3:00 p.m., I received a phone call advising me that my PSA (prostate-specific antigen) blood test came back at 8.9. A PSA level between four and ten usually indicates a 25 percent chance of prostate cancer. I have always considered myself a positive person—positive, but realistic. I cannot begin to tell you how hard it is to stay positive on this journey. As I sit here once again on July 12, trying to chronicle this journey, I'm waiting for a call from the urologist. Once again life has been put on hold.

CHAPTER 12

REFLECTIONS—"CALIFORNIA, HERE I COME," JULY 1978

The office in Los Angeles had made my reservations for my arrival at my new assignment. For the near future I would be calling the Century Plaza Hotel my home. I arrived on a Sunday afternoon, and after checking in, I decided to see whether I could find my new office. It was located across the plaza from the hotel; this was the shortest commute to my office I would experience in my career.

I can still feel the sense of accomplishment and excitement as I stood in the office looking out over the plaza. There was a free concert in the plaza featuring a relatively new performer by the name of Olivia Newton-John. I remember scanning the bars and restaurants surrounding the plaza when my eye caught the familiar logo ears of the Playboy Club of LA. For a country boy from Saukville, Wisconsin, what better symbol of reaching some level of success could I expect? I had become a member when they opened the Playboy Club in Lake Geneva. Now I walked across the plaza to use my card for the first time in years.

I was disappointed to learn that they did not sell Miller products. I explained to the manager that I had just been transferred here from the East Coast, and since my office was across the street, I planned on spending a lot of time at the club, but I couldn't justify it if they didn't sell my products. She smiled and told me to send the salesman by and I could be assured that I would be able to get Miller beer the next time I stopped by.

As I left the club, I was happy that I had been able to place Miller products in the Playboy Club but couldn't help but wonder why the people working out of this office had been unable to do it before I got there.

And so began the new culture that would be introduced to the Miller employees in Southern California. "Ask for the order. If the boss has to do it, why does he need you?" There were a lot of levels of management between me and the ultimate consumer. Slowly the network began to become more sales oriented.

In the past the culture could be described as composed of order takers, not sellers. Now the performers would be recognized and rewarded. Those that didn't respond would eventually be replaced. No one wanted to be embarrassed when I or one of our management team walked into a bar and was not able to get our products. No one wanted to be asked the question, Why could the boss place the product but not the salesman?

Miller's relocation policy was very generous. While staying at the Century Plaza Hotel was very convenient, it was also very expensive. Relocation into the most expensive real estate market was also hard on those of us in the process. As I was rebuilding our sales force in Southern California, many of us shared our hardships because of relocation. The interest rate on the house I would eventually purchase in Redondo Beach was 14 percent. The company had an interest rate differential whereby they made up the difference between the rate I was paying on my old house before relocation and my new interest rate. My interest rate in Washington, DC, was 7 percent, so the company reimbursed me the additional 7 percent.

Before settling into my house in Redondo Beach, I moved around LA and Santa Monica to learn the area. One of the hotels I called home for a while was the Marriott in Marina Del Rey. More days than not I would have to pinch myself to be sure I was not dreaming and still living back in Saukville, Wisconsin.

One morning while exiting the hotel on my way to work, I was greeted by a movie production group that was setting up for a shoot. There were people all over the parking lot and lobby. There were cameramen, portable lights, and makeup people running around responding to several people giving orders with bullhorns. At first, I was unsure what was happening, but as I scanned the actors and extras, it became obvious when I recognized the actresses of *Charlie's Angels*. Wow. Saukville had never been like this, but I would soon learn that life in LA was different from in any place I had ever lived.

There was a bar named the Rangoon Racquet Club on Little Santa Monica in Beverly Hills, which was a short distance from our office. It had nothing to do with racket sports but was a favorite of many locals and some of our senior management from Milwaukee when they would come to town for meetings. I recall one such evening. When we arrived, there was a bigger crowd than usual developing at the bar. It didn't take long for us to determine that the reason for the crowd was two of the patrons at the bar, who were recognizable to just about anyone who didn't live under a rock.

For the next hour, those of us who were lucky enough to position ourselves close enough to the action were entertained by Ed McMahon and Betty White. They were doing stand-up comedy, telling stories that appeared to be personal stories about themselves and other celebrities in funny situations. I am not exaggerating, but they had the people at the bar in stitches for at least an hour. And they treated those of us lucky enough to be close by like we were old friends and equals. Not always the case in Hollywood, but it was with these two. And unsurprisingly, Betty White had never heard of Saukville.

Needless to say, I loved LA. My territory was unbelievable for a thirty-something single guy trying to build a career. Another of my favorite bars in the LA area was the "Ginger Man" in Beverly Hills. It was a fun place and a favorite of some of the celebrities—it was owned by Carroll O'Connor and Patrick O'Neal. Carroll O'Connor played Archie Bunker in the popular TV series *All in the Family* in the late seventies. Archie played the part of a bigoted working-class family man. Great series for its time. Today the "woke" crowd would probably firebomb the bar. So sad.

The rest of my territory consisted of Southern California to the Mexican border, obviously including San Diego; all of Arizona; Las Vegas, Nevada; and the state of Hawaii. Looking back, I think living in LA was like a four-year college course in life. I used to say walking into my office was like walking into the United Nations. Because of the diversity of LA and the nature of our business, we needed to have a presence in all segments of the market. Obviously, even back in the late seventies and early eighties, the Hispanic market was the largest. The African American market was also very large, as well as the Asian market. It is so unfortunate that today some ignorant and relatively uninformed people and politicians have chosen to use racism as a tool for divisiveness.

Being responsible for Hawaii also taught me a lot about bigotry and racism. It didn't take long for me to learn that the locals did not like the typical American tourist. They loved the money that came from the tourism industry but not the people. I learned very soon that you never referred to the United States as "back in the States" but rather as "on the mainland." The term "haole" was how they referred to white people, with about the same meaning as the N-word in our lexicon today. Hawaii was a very desirable post for our sales force until they were assigned there. It would usually take about six to eight months for them to plead with me to get them off the rock. I would venture to say that anyone that may have some racist tendencies prior to being assigned to Hawaii got over them very quickly once they were on the receiving side of bigotry.

CHAPTER 13

REFLECTIONS OF AN UNDERCOVER MAN

The beer business is closely regulated by the federal and state governments. After the elimination of Prohibition in 1933, the federal government established the Bureau of Alcohol, Tobacco, and Firearms for the express purpose of monitoring and controlling the sale and consumption of alcoholic beverages. Tied house laws were instituted as one of the tools the government would use. They were established to prohibit brewers, distillers, winegrowers, and other alcoholic-beverage suppliers from exerting undue influence over retailers. Threats to the existence of one's business replaced threats from Al Capone and the mafia.

One of the features of the tied house laws was that a brewer could not pay for business in return for exclusivity. During my stint in LA, there came a time when I was called back to Milwaukee for a meeting to discuss business. In that meeting I advised our management that while we were observing both the letter of the law and spirit of the law, our primary competition, Anheuser-Busch (A/B), was not. We were virtually shut out of many large venues, such as Los Angeles's Dodger Stadium and others. A/B would buy the TV advertising sponsorship for the team, and in return they would get exclusive beer distribution in the park for their brands of beer, virtually locking out all competitors. It was illegal.

In my meeting with the management, I told them that we were competing with one hand behind our back. They were reluctant at first to believe me when I said that what A/B was doing was illegal and that it didn't seem to be stopping them. I implied that if they didn't believe me, maybe someone in a management position should get out of the ivory tower and see what was really happening in the field.

When Philip Morris bought Miller, the industry had some corrupt practices left over from the Prohibition days. Philip Morris made a $2 million offer as a compromise when it purchased Miller and promised not to participate in anything illegal going forward. A/B made no such arrangement. Several months after my meeting with management, I received a call from the senior legal counsel advising me that I would be getting a visit from an agent of ATF (Alcohol, Tobacco, and Firearms) as a follow-up to my accusation that A/B was breaking the law. The senior counsel didn't say it, but what was obvious in our conversation was an attitude of "here you go, smart-ass. If you're going to make an accusation, this is your time to prove it."

In a few days, I received a call from the agent. We decided he would just accompany me on sales calls as another Miller rep in training. My persistence paid off. Even though I knew the Dodgers would not put in our beer, I had been calling them relentlessly. The food and beverage manager respected my persistence, and when I called him, he would even joke about how he really liked me and wished he could put in the beer but it was out of his hands unless we bought the advertising. My hope was that he would say something similar in front of the ATF guy. Well, when the time came and I was making my call in the presence of the government agent, he did. Months later we would learn that A/B would pay a $20 million fine for past wrongdoings and promise to clean up their act going forward.

After leaving the Dodgers' office, I called my office for messages. Before cell phones, the only way we could stay on top of business was to check in with the office frequently. This time my secretary advised me that a Mr. Steve Wozniak had called and left a message for me to call him regarding beer for an upcoming rock concert. I'm ashamed to admit that I didn't know who this Wozniak was, but "Mr. Secret Agent Man" did and advised me that, along with Mr. Steve Jobs, he was the cofounder of Apple Computer Company.

GUT PUNCH

While I would have preferred to have made the sales call to Mr. Wozniak without the supervision of an ATF representative, I had no choice. Soon we were sitting in front of one of the most successful businessmen in the world, listening to him tell us about his dream of creating one of the biggest and most inclusive rock concerts to date. My assumption was that since he probably missed Woodstock because he was too busy studying computer science, he wanted to create his own.

He described his vision of having a weeklong concert featuring different types of music—rock, jazz, country, and other genres—each day, with the stars of the various genres featured each day. It would be billed as the largest concert in history and labeled the US Concert, to be the most inclusive of all music festivals. When I heard that Willie Nelson would headline the country music day, I just knew we had to be the beer featured. In addition to Willie, other performers included Fleetwood Mac, the Police, Tom Petty, Santana, Jimmy Buffett, the Grateful Dead, and the Kinks. We had a brewery located near the festival site, in Irwindale, California, so I knew that servicing the venue would be facilitated by our location.

WAYLON JENNINGS

I have been a country music fan for as long as I can remember. I was a Willie fan when he had short black hair and wore a suit for his performances. You can imagine my pleasure as I sat backstage watching Willie perform and knew that in a small way, I was a part of the concert. There were folding chairs reserved for VIPs set up off to the side, where we wouldn't be visible to the audience. And here was that kid from Saukville sitting about fifty feet from Willie Nelson.

One of the unexpected surprises was when some of the stagehands began to scramble and do whatever stagehands do. They were whispering in low voices, saying, "Hey, he plans on walking right onstage while Willie's playing. He is also higher than a kite." We soon realized that "he" was none other than Waylon Jennings, another very popular country star of the time. He waited until Willie completed the song he was performing; then he slowly passed within twenty feet of us with his guitar slung over his back. Willie saw him approach and acknowledged his presence. Waylon then said, "Evening, Willie. You mind if I join you for a song or two?" and with that they did a few duets and completed the show. I left the backstage area and headed home at about midnight but heard the next morning that Willie had continued to play until almost 2:00 a.m. This was 1982 and I now had been selling Miller beer for about ten years. If my career had stopped then, I would have considered it to be very rewarding. My time in California rewarded me with some of the best friendships I could have ever imagined. Beer sales in the region continued to accelerate, and I continued to take advantage of the California lifestyle. With Hawaii and Las Vegas also in my territory, there was never a lack of interesting activities when I wasn't working.

OFFSHORE FISHING IN CABO

SKIING ON LAKE MEAD

The good news was that because of the nature of our industry, I could often combine business with pleasure. As a teenager I was an avid water-skier on the inland lakes of southeastern Wisconsin. Now I was able to expand that experience in Southern California and Lake Mead in Nevada. I took up snow skiing and learned the basics in Mammoth Lakes, California. Mammoth Lakes is a town in California's Sierra Nevada. It's known for the Mammoth Mountain and June Mountain ski areas and nearby trails. Close to home was Big Bear Mountain in Southern California, where my new local friends and I would go for weekend getaways.

My boating interests were also addressed once again because of location. I soon learned that some of the best sport fishing was in Cabo San Lucas in the Mexican Baja. A short flight from LA, and we were in some of the best marlin and sailfish water in the world. I might add that when I went to Cabo, it was nothing like it is today. Back then there was one dirt road that led to the marina. Today it is a thriving metropolis in the Mexican Baja. Closer to home there was great boating between our coast and Catalina Island.

If it hasn't become apparent by now, the beer industry provided many opportunities to party, and party we did. I recall a pool party at my house in Redondo Beach. One of the guys I recruited from my old office in Washington, DC, to help me in California was a good guitar player. While walking on Venice Beach, he came across a banjo player playing for tips. Turns out the guy was a gemologist and simply playing for tips on the beach for a hoot. Well, my friend brought him along to the party. Later we learned that he and my friend were playing in a bluegrass competition called the Topanga Canyon Fiddle and Banjo Competition taking place at the UCLA infield the next day. So a bunch of us decided to load up our coolers and head for the bluegrass competition the next day to give them moral support and biased applause.

While sitting in lawn chairs watching the competition and drinking beer, I found myself getting jealous. They looked like they were having so much fun. How hard could it be to play a guitar? The next day at work, I asked my friend if he would help me buy a guitar and learn how to play. I'm not sure today whether he did it because I was the boss or whether he was just a nice guy and felt sorry for me, but nonetheless, by the end of the day I was the proud owner of a Gibson six-string acoustic guitar and had learned the finger placement for three chords. I would practice those three chords every night when I got home from work until I mastered them.

But I soon realized that playing guitar was more than three chords. I took lessons from a guitar teacher in Manhattan Beach whenever I could fit it in my schedule, but it turned out to be a longer process that I originally thought. I soon learned the answer to my question, "How hard can it be?"—especially once you were over the age of thirty. Over time I got to learn a few more chords and realized how hard it was.

While I was mastering the three-chord progression, my friend told me that he and his banjo friend were signing up for the bluegrass festival again, and now they had a fiddle player and a stand-up bass player as well. He wanted me to play rhythm guitar and help out with the vocals. I damn near died. He told me I would only have to learn two more chords, and I had a couple of months to practice. With some reluctance, I said, "What the hell, I'll give it a try." To make a long story tolerable, it was a blast. We won second prize, which was one guitar strap, and had a great time drinking beer on the infield of UCLA—and I got as close to being an entertainer as I ever will.

There is no question in my mind that my territory was a dream, and once we got some of the business problems resolved, it became more and more enjoyable to live there. I always said that if I ever had to leave, I would one day return to retire there. Looking back, it saddens me to see what bad politics and bad state government have done to ruin one of the nicest places in God's creation.

CHAPTER 14

REFLECTIONS ON WHAT YOU WISH FOR

Me with the best boss I ever had, L. J. Goldstein, president and CEO of Miller Brewing Co.

By 1984 I was promoted to senior vice president of sales and relocated back to the corporate headquarters in Milwaukee. The adjustment wasn't easy. First, I had not seen snow, with the exception of skiing on it, in over seven years. Second, I went from an environment where I had complete autonomy and independence, with no one looking over my shoulder, to working in the corporate fishbowl. I can recall on several occasions thinking what a mistake I made. What had I done? What was I thinking?

I can say now that at the time of my promotion the field sales force was, I believe, among the best in the industry. I was surrounded by some of the hardest working, conscientious and creative people in the work force. We had the diversity back then that everyone talks about today. Without them I would never have achieved the status I did. I regret never being able to tell them how much I appreciated their efforts before I left.

I now had use of the company plane. As I look back, I think I spent half of my life in the air. It sure was a lot nicer flying in our own plane. While on the surface it may look like a luxury—and I won't deny it was—it also allowed me to visit distributors that it would have otherwise take me days to get to. Distributors who had been Miller distributors for years told me that I was the first member of Miller's senior management team ever to come and visit them in their markets.

GUT PUNCH

As I climbed the ladder, my management style continued to evolve, but some core principles remained the same. I would frequently call a distributor and tell him that I would be arriving the next day and would appreciate it if I could ride a truck with one of the driver salesmen. What? This was unheard of. A senior VP of Miller riding a beer truck: Are you kidding me? They were also put in a difficult spot. First, they didn't want me to be out there riding alone with one of their people unsupervised. They couldn't tell me that they needed more lead time because they had trucks on the road every day, so many times they would have to change their schedule to accompany me on sales calls to their customers if they didn't want me out there alone with their customers. It was amazing what I learned. Did they know their customers' names? Did they have a good relationship with their customers? Did they have a service problem that was unresolved?

It was during Ronald Reagan's presidency that he told an audience that the nine most dreaded words for anyone to hear were "I'm from the government, and I'm here to help." During one of the national sales meetings, I took the liberty to make a slight change to the famous Reagan quote, amending it to "I'm from the brewery, and I'm here to help." It got a tremendous laugh, but the word would spread quickly that when Tom came to visit, the last question you wanted to answer was "If I have to sell it, why do I need you?"

Leading by example became another pillar of my management style. I served as senior VP of sales from 1984 to 1994. Miller sales and market share continued to grow—however, each year at a slightly slower rate. Early in the growth curve, we introduced an incentive program for our distributors that was truly amazing. It was called the Miller Masters. As you might imagine, the truly successful distributors were very financially secure. We created an incentive contest for the top ten or twelve distributors that demonstrated the best business practices in our company. The reward was a trip to one part of the world that they would never take for themselves. As part of the senior management team, I was automatically included in the prize.

There were many memorable trips, like a trip on the Orient Express across Scandinavia or a trip to the Royal Ascot in Great Britain, which allowed me to experience my one and only flight on the Concorde. Flying from London to New York in just under three hours was an amazing experience. The plane had four Rolls-Royce engines with afterburners to propel it through liftoff and the sound barrier, or Mach 1—a speed of 662 nautical miles per hour at sea level or 1,354 nautical miles per hour right to the edge of the space. The only way to describe the experience back then was to call it futuristic. With ticket prices at $1,200 round trip, it was a pretty safe bet that the distributors would not be buying one for themselves any time soon—although you did get champagne and caviar for starters and lobster or duck à l'orange for the entrée. No movies, just a Mach display showing speed and altitude. At fifty-five thousand feet, you could see the curvature of the earth.

GUT PUNCH

However, the most memorable trip for me was an African safari to the Mount Kenya Safari Club. One of the highlights of the African safari was being able to see a Maasai village. The Maasai are a Nilotic ethnic group inhabiting northern, central, and southern Kenya and northern Tanzania. They are among the best-known local populations internationally due to their residence near the many game parks and their distinctive customs and dress.

The morning we chose to visit the Maasai village, our driver pointed out a rather large black cloud off in the distance. It did not appear to be weather related but rather a dust cloud that hung over what we assumed to be the village off in the distance. As we approached, the driver explained that the cloud we were observing consisted of flies. Millions of flies hovered over the village. He explained that the Maasai built their huts out of tree branches and other natural vegetation found in the area. They then used cow dung applied to the outside to waterproof the individual huts. The fly infestation was unbelievable. You either kept your mouth shut while in the village or you couldn't help but inhale or swallow them. As I approached one of the huts, a woman was breastfeeding a baby outside the door to the hut while the flies were crawling around the baby's mouth. The hut I entered had small open fire in the middle. There were no flies inside the hut. I imagine it was because of the open fire with no chimney.

GUT PUNCH

The Maasai go back over six hundred years and have not changed or picked up any elements of modern society during that time. The men tend to the livestock, and the women take care of the children and do the cooking. Because they are nomadic, they move constantly to locations that can support the livestock. When they move, the men move the herds while the women pack up the huts and belongings and carry them on their heads to the new location. Needless to say, there was much discussion about the role of women in society at the cocktail hour that evening.

Throughout the eighties business continued to grow. Miller's operating philosophy in the seventies and eighties was innovation supported by superior marketing and advertising. Unfortunately, the flagship brand, Miller High Life, was losing steam. Although it had a loyal following, sales continued to decline.

CHAPTER 15

REFLECTIONS ON A FUN WORK ENVIRONMENT

The "Cold Patrol"

Consistent with our philosophy of innovation, we introduced a new product in the mid-1980s called Miller Genuine Draft. It was not pasteurized and utilized the advertising hook of being cold filtered. It was supported by great advertising and in-market promotion to emphasis the cold-filtered concept at the local level. Miller distributors supported "cold patrols" that used models to make sales and promotion calls at the retail level. How could anyone say no to this crew? And they didn't. For the Lite brand, we used retired professional athletes called the Lite All-Stars. They were as crazy to work with as they appeared to be in the commercials.

Through the end of the eighties, sales continued to improve. We had good advertising for the three brands, but soon the campaigns began to get old. Try as the agencies might, they were unable to freshen up the campaigns. They say timing is everything, and at the same time that our campaigns were getting old, Coors decided to introduce their products into the remainder of the United States. Prior to 1987 Coors sold beer only west of the Mississippi River. To make matters worse, they almost exclusively chose the Miller distributors to sell their beer. The distributors did their best to provide equal emphasis to both brands, but the beer consumer was infatuated with this new brand that was previously unavailable to them and in many cases available to them only when they vacationed west. By the early nineties, Coors had successfully eroded the business of the two major brewers and began to set the stage for the final stage of the beer-industry consolidation. There just wasn't enough total volume to support the remaining brewers. By 1990 A/B had a 43 percent share, while Miller had a 22 percent share and Coors was approaching 10 percent, but the pressure was growing.

MY FIRST SAILBOAT, *THE HIGH LIFE*

GUT PUNCH

For most of my life in the beer business, I was focused on business, with little time left over for anything else. With two divorces and not much of a personal life, one night while leaving the corporate office, I decided that I was going to do something for myself before the summer was over. I had always wanted to learn how to sail, so before the week was over, I was signed up for a sailing lesson at the Milwaukee Community Sailing Center. That introduction to the boating world provided me with a lifetime pastime second only to snow skiing.

Eventually I put together a team of local guys with a similar interest in sailing. We competed in the Queen's Cup, which was a race across Lake Michigan from Milwaukee to Muskegon. We came in second one year, which was offset by my coming in dead last in the Chicago/Mac, the granddaddy of sailboat races on Lake Michigan, a year later.

On one of the few days I was in the office; I received a phone call from a friend who worked at an advertising agency in town informing me that they were planning to have a helicopter in the sky late afternoon and early evening. They were planning on getting some footage for an ad they were creating for the city of Milwaukee. He knew I had a custom-made spinnaker with the classic "Lady in the Moon" Miller High Life logo. He said, "If you want some free publicity, I suggest you have your boat out in the harbor this afternoon."

Exposure means sales, and naturally I would be there. I immediately called the crew and started a telephone tree to be sure to have enough help on board. When I arrived, the crew was on board. I was the last to arrive, as usual. One of the guys who was a far better sailor than I was had the boat running at the dock. All I had to do was go below and change out of my business suit. He ran the boat while I grabbed a beer as we navigated our way away from the dock and out into open water. Once we were on our way and heading out of the main harbor, my friend looked up and said, "Shit, skipper, I didn't see him" as we both looked up to see a UWM racing team boat bounce off our starboard side. It had been hidden from our view by our genoa. Looking back, it was simple. We had so many people on board that everyone thought everyone else was keeping a lookout, but no one was. I called out to the racing team to see that they were uninjured and there had been no damage. They replied that they were all OK, but they were quick to advise me that my boat wasn't. They said it looked like I had a hole right above the waterline. I immediately sent someone down below to confirm that yes, we were taking on water. We immediately changed our tack so that the hull in question would be out of the water. Doing so, we were able to assess the damage and determined that yes, we did have a hole in the hull just above the waterline.

Since we had some of the girlfriends of the crew members on board, we asked for a volunteer to be hung over the side and held by the ankles to dry off the area in question. Once it was dry, we repaired the area in question with, yup, you guessed it, duct tape. Inside the cabin, at the area of the hole, we placed cushions, with crew members applying pressure from the inside. We brought the boat about to check on the worthiness of our repair. Satisfied that it was holding, we directed all available hands on the deck to sit with their legs hanging over the side to cover the duct tape patch. We popped the spinnaker and sailed back into the harbor to the sounds of the helicopter overhead. Satisfied that we had been able to get all the film footage available to us, we motored back to the dock to arrange for repairs. We were lucky that the hole was right above the waterline and that when the boat was stable and not under sail, the boat did not take on water.

One of the crew members knew a fiberglass guy and called him. Luckily, he was available and came to the boat to assess the damage and begin repairs. As we were planning on taking the boat to Chicago the next day for the weekend, there was much discussion about whether or not we would still be able to make the trip. The fiberglass guy was sure there would be no problem making a suitable seaworthy patch, but if you have ever worked with fiberglass, you know that the mess remaining after the repair would be harder work to clean up than creating the original patch. We decided to let the fiberglass guy do his work, and the rest of us would regroup in the morning and determine whether we could still get the boat ready for the trip.

Bright and early the next morning, several of us arrived at the dock to determine the amount of work remaining in order to get the boat ready for our trip to Chicago. We were shocked to see that the boat had been cleaned, and while some minor things needed to be done, we could take our trip if we still desired to do so. I called the fiberglass guy to inquire whether he had done the cleaning, because he'd made it clear that while he would do the patch work, cleaning was not part of the deal. He informed me that there had been an older guy hanging around the boat who had volunteered to help after we all left the night before. He said that he was still cleaning up after he finished the patch work and headed home. He said he thought the guy's name was Bob. He smoked a corncob pipe and usually hung around the docks during the day.

Later that day, I saw a man smoking a corncob pipe walking down the dock, heading to our boat. I asked him whether he was the mysterious cleaning phantom and learned that he indeed was. He said he had overheard us talking about our planned trip, and since he didn't have anything better to do, he just stuck around and cleaned up the boat. Wow. I invited him to join us and also tried to pay him for the work he did. He refused both. I learned he was a disabled Korean War vet. He said that he enjoyed being near the boats and the shores of Lake Michigan. In the summer months, he said, he would get up early, take the bus down to the lakefront, and just hang out.

I asked him whether he would like a job cleaning my boat once per week. The only time I could use the boat was on weekends, and spending a half day cleaning it on Saturday morning before I took it out was getting old. He agreed, and I told him to check with me the next week after we returned from Chicago. He did, and I hired him to wash the boat when weather permitted so that it would be ready for me to use on the weekend.

The following Saturday I arrived at the boat and found the boat the cleanest I had ever observed—certainly cleaner than anytime I had cleaned it. I asked Bob how much I owed him, and he simply shrugged his shoulders, saying he had no idea what to charge. I then asked him how much time he'd spent working on the boat, and he said that since it took him a long time to do things, he had started working on it sometime Thursday morning so it would be ready for me on Saturday. I had no intention of paying him for three days of work for something that should have taken three or four hours. I told him that the going rate from a cleaning service was about twenty-five dollars, but since he had done such a great job, I would pay him thirty, and I didn't care if he decided to start a day or two in advance to get the job done if it was done by Saturday mornings.

I was shocked when he told me he would have done it for free. He said he used to come down to the harbor and sit on picnic benches, staring at the boats. He said he would always look at my boat and dream about what it would be like to sail on it. I would learn in time that Bob was a formerly homeless person who used to live on the streets of Los Angeles. He eventually worked his way to the Midwest because he wanted to be near the VA hospital in Milwaukee. He told me his real desire was to be near the VA hospital in Saint Petersburg, Florida, because he'd heard it was one of the best in the country. He said he lived off his VA benefits—not much, but enough to cover the room he rented because the Wisconsin climate was too brutal to live on the streets.

From that point on, Bob became a semipermanent resident on *High Life*. He was a very private person. If we had a large group going sailing, he would usually opt to stay on shore. If, however, it was just me or a small group, he would join us. Often, he and I would sail to either Racine or Kenosha for a weekend, or sometimes we would sail north to Port Washington to visit my parents. While I could handle the forty-one-foot sloop by myself, it was always easier with at least one other crew member.

CHAPTER 16

REFLECTIONS ON MY ROCKY MOUNTAIN HIGH

Over my twenty-plus-year career at Miller, I was able to live through some of the best times to be in the beer industry. I developed close friendships with a lot of locals in Vail, including a ski instructor. I ultimately hired him to represent Miller beer on the mountain, and as such we were able to develop and attend many on-mountain promotions over the years. We participated in bartender cup races and, most notably, the Jerry Ford Downhill Classic.

President Ford began bringing his family to Vail in 1968 and soon bought a home there. With a footballer's tender knees, he stayed on groomed terrain but skied aggressively enough to fall hard occasionally. After his presidency he built a house in Beaver Creek. We could easily see the Secret Service agents at their posts, surrounding the residence. He helped promote a variety of charities around the valley, creating the Jerry Ford Invitational golf tournament. In 1982 he established the Ford Cup, the ski race that eventually became the American Ski Classic. He continued to race in celebrity events until his knees forced his retirement from the sport in 1984.

President Ford's involvement in the Vail Valley resulted in significant contributions in many areas, and the community paid him back by naming the outdoor theater the Ford Amphitheater. One of my most memorable skiing memories occurred at one of the American Ski Classic events I attended. Friends of mine and I were sitting at a table having beers and watching President Ford sign autographs when my friend Mark, the ski instructor who now worked for us, came up to me and whispered in my ear, "Get your skis and follow me." I did as I was instructed and followed him outside only to be joined by Franz Klammer and Franz Weber. For those unfamiliar with the sport, Franz Klammer was the 1972 Olympic downhill gold medal winner from Austria, and Franz Weber was the fastest man on skis. I believe he still holds the North American record at just under 130 miles per hour. They were both in town to compete in the Jerry Ford American Ski Classic with other active and retired ski celebrities. It was a pro-am event brought to Vail by President Ford as a fundraiser for the US ski team.

GUT PUNCH

Mark relished the look on my face when he told me we were making a run with Franz and Franz. We jumped on the chairlift right next to the hospitality tent, which dropped at the top of a run called Centennial. The first part of the run was intermediate, but as you got closer to the bottom, it turned into an expert run. I had never experienced such an emotion that put a smile on my face from ear to ear. Here I was, the kid from Saukville, going down a ski run following the fastest man on skis while being followed by an Olympic gold medal winner. God, I loved my job.

Later that evening we had an impromptu pizza party at my condo. Not to be a name dropper, but present, in addition to Franz and Franz, was American gold medal winner Billy Johnson. I know there were others, but my memory is a little fuzzy. Maybe had something to do with the quantities of beer and pizza that were consumed.

As I think back to the many memories of my time in the beer business, one of my most cherished occurred shortly after being relocated back to Milwaukee. One of my dearest friends managed the Miller distributorship in Sylmar, California, a suburb of LA. He called me one day to tell me that he had recently run into Willie Nelson and Gene Autry at his country club. He said he told Willie the story I used to tell about how if I ever had the chance to meet Willie, I would have him autograph my guitar with a nail. I was his biggest fan. I liked him even before he had long hair and a beard. My friend said, "Tom, I'm not sure if he will call you or not, but he asked for your phone number at work and said he would call."

At the time I had two secretaries, and it was about the time voice mail was just becoming popular. I summoned both of my secretaries and told them that I knew it was easy to send my phone calls to voice mail when they weren't at their desks, but for the next couple of months, if I found out that a call from Willie Nelson had been sent to voice mail, I would fire them both on the spot.

Several weeks passed, and one day I was in an advertising meeting in the boardroom when my secretary peeked her head in the back door and said. "Mr. Koehler, Willie Nelson is on line one for you." While I almost peed my pants, I can still feel the proud smile on my face as I got up and excused myself to take the call. We had about a half-hour conversation about how I was a big fan and so humbled that he'd actually called me. He told me not to get too excited because he had a business reason for calling as well. He was thinking about starting a satellite radio station, and would we be willing to buy some advertising? I responded that we certainly would consider it and also made arrangements to send him a Miller Lite–branded golf bag because I knew he was a big golfer. With a big shit-eating grin, I returned to the boardroom to continue the meeting. It was probably one of my best moments of working in corporate America.

CHAPTER 17

REFLECTIONS ON THE BEST AND THE WORST OF TIMES

While I worked at Miller for some of the best times, I was also there for the not-so-good times. The culture slowly changed. As people grew older, there were retirements, in addition to the new senior executives who came aboard with the acquisitions that Philip Morris made along the way. Where once there had been no politics, it now raised its ugly head.

While I was vice president of sales, I worked for five different presidents. The first, John Murphy, established the culture. The third, Leonard Goldstein was able to positively accelerate the original culture. The fifth and last one came from within the industry and had an extensive background, but in my opinion the culture he came from was not compatible with that of current day Miller . From the beginning I could feel the target on my back.

In an effort to dress up the bride before Philip Morris sold Miller, consultants had been brought in. BCG, Boston Consulting Group, founded by Mitt Romney, was the first. It was about that time that I received a phone call from a headhunter. I could tell they were feeling me out about an opportunity with another company. I was willing to explore any opportunity. We had been communicating for several months when one morning I received a phone call in which I was advised that the company interested in me was prepared to make an offer.

During this same period, the BCG consultants were occupying so much of our time that we didn't have time for our regular jobs, and business

95

suffered. While they were nice folks, they were not beer people. They came in armed with their MBAs and were prepared to change the world. Their recommendations would do little to improve the condition of Miller and, one might add, possibly made things worse. The final call from the headhunter came in the midst of the BCG project. He informed me that the company that was interested in me had made their final decision and that the job was mine if I wanted it. The company was the Barton Beer Company, one of two importers representing Corona in the United States. They were offering me the position of president. I spent several sleepless nights considering the offer before I had to make a decision. Because of the nature of the job, I was not able to discuss it with any close confidants; they all worked at Miller. After twenty-plus years at Miller, I finally decided that moving to another company in the beer business was too much for my loyalty to withstand and turned down the offer. I decided that the current pressure created by BCG would eventually go away and there was a chance we could return to normalcy, and I would not cut a run but stick it out.

Over the next several months, the conditions did not get any better. The new president and I clearly did not work well together. The longer we worked together, the less I respected his abilities or him as an individual. We argued on many occasions, until the last time, when he presented me with my letter of resignation. I'll never forget that. I had been at the hospital that morning with my mother, who was undergoing colon surgery. The surgery, which was supposed to be routine because she had recently received the news that the tumor was benign, turned out to be very extensive. While the area where the biopsy was done was benign, the surrounding area was filled with cancer. As I sat across from the president later that day, he asked where I had been that morning. I told him I had been at the hospital because my mother was undergoing cancer surgery. He asked how she was doing, and when I answered that she had about three months to live, he simply shrugged and without skipping a beat handed me my letter of resignation to sign. Twenty-plus years of loyalty, and all he could do was shrug.

They say God works in strange ways. As a result of my terminated employment, I was able to spend time with my mom. This would never have been possible if I had been working. I would not have been able to take the time off. I spent every possible hour with her; many nights we would sleep together. I would hold her in my arms while we both cried ourselves to sleep.

I did receive a very fair severance package. However, it was subject to a noncompete clause. While I received an immediate offer to go to work for Coors, they withdrew it as a result of the clause. I asked them to give me a chance to resolve it before they made their final decision, but they said they didn't want to get into any litigation with Miller.

I did receive some satisfaction. When the president asked me to resign, Miller Brewing had a 22 percent share of market. When the company was finally sold, under his direction, the market share had fallen to 16 percent. Guess I wasn't so bad after all.

CHAPTER 18

REFLECTIONS ON CHANGE

Just as the beer industry was going through a period of consolidation, so too was the soft drink industry. A venture capital firm by the name of Hicks Muse had successfully consolidated 7UP, Dr. Pepper, and A&W Root Beer. The same company was trying to do the same thing with the beer industry. Stroh, Pabst, and Heileman were prime for consolidation, and Hicks Muse had already purchased Heileman. I was hired by them to take over the sales at Heileman and assist in the acquisition and consolidation of the three companies. If the consolidation strategy worked as it did in the soft drink industry, I would never again have to worry about money. Once again, a new journey and an opportunity to reinvent myself for the second time at the ripe old age of forty-six.

Forty-six is not the ideal age to be starting a new career, but my choices were few. All my experience was in the beer industry, and not many companies' human resources departments were willing to take the risk on me, especially when there were many young people out there with more desirable skill sets. I felt I was lucky to get the opportunity.

Up until this time, my experience was primarily in sales and marketing. My new position was inclusive of all areas of the business, including production, pricing, distribution, and finance. I can honestly say that I learned more about business while working for the venture capital group than at any other time in my career.

The working environment was like nothing I had ever experience before. The managing partner group had its office in the sky. They had a Gulfstream

IV, and although we had small offices in Chicago, we were hardly ever there. Rather, we were traveling to distributorships around the United States so the new group could learn the business.

Shortly after going to work for Hicks Muse, the venture capital group, I received a call from an old friend in the sailing industry and who had most recently been involved in the beer business in Russia. When I was at Miller, I was instrumental in helping his group acquire Miller beer to import to Russia. His group had asked me to be on their board; however, when I requested permission from Miller senior management, it was refused. When I requested permission this time, it was granted immediately. The Hicks Muse management philosophy was very similar to what I had become accustomed to when first hired at Miller. This permission included time off from my normal responsibilities at Heileman to periodically travel to Russia to assist the new group. Naturally the Russian group would be selling Heileman products as well.

Currently, I was spending as much time with my mom as possible, but I did commit to several trips to Moscow. By this time my dad also needed long-term care and was in a nursing home. The plan had been to bring him home after my mom's so-called routine surgery. I needed someone to look after them when I was in Russia, so on one of my sailing trips with Bob, my Korean War vet friend, I suggested that perhaps he should move in with them to be my eyes and ears when I wasn't around. I had already told Bob that he could move out of his rooming house and stay with my mom if she agreed. I told my mom she should talk to Bob about the idea while I made a fictitious trip to the grocery store and liquor store. When I returned, she advised me that Bob was moving in. Without having to pay for his room in Milwaukee, and with groceries on my mom and dad's budget, Bob would be saving money for the first time in his life.

Working for Heileman in conjunction with Hicks Muse was very exciting and very interesting. But it soon became obvious that Hicks Muse had paid too much for Heileman and that either we would have to buy one of the other breweries quickly at the right price or we would need to sell Heileman. The management team met for a strategy session that would ultimately result in the sale of Heileman to Stroh.

It was truly an example of businessman chess. the objective of the meeting with Stroh was to go in trying to convince them that we wanted to buy them, knowing full well that we in fact wanted to unload Heileman. After our team leader made a very convincing presentation on the acquisition, the president of Stroh turned the table and said he wanted to buy us. While we all had our surprise game face on, I'm surprised that the jubilation on the plane back to Chicago couldn't be heard in Detroit.

The surprise move by Stroh to purchase Heileman was, I believe, more of an emotional decision than a business decision. Being the last family business among the major breweries to be purchased by an outside company was too much for the family to bear. Nonetheless, the purchase was too much for Stroh to absorb financially, and this was the first domino to fall. Pabst, Stroh, and Heileman brands were then split up between Miller, A/B, and Coors. The final phase of consolidation came when InBev purchased A/B and Molson Coors merged with Miller. This all occurred while the American beer industry was giving birth to the new age of craft beers and hundreds of microbreweries were popping up all over the country. When I look back, I realize I was in the beer business during the best time to be in the beer business.

As part of the Heileman sales agreement, I was hired as an outside consultant to Stroh to assist in consolidating their distribution system. The journey continued with a slight detour. At the same time, I began to see the Russian operation as a potential gold mine. I could satisfy my responsibilities consulting for Stroh as well as increase my time assisting the Russian venture.

It took about a year for me to realize that my time spent consulting for Stroh was not very rewarding. I would do the projects and make the recommendations, and they would just sit on someone's desk, never to be implemented. I was making the same amount of money working about fifteen days a month as I was when on salary. However, my recommendations were never acted on. I told them in one of my meetings that I really thought they were wasting their money by having consultants to make recommendations that were never implemented. The then-president thanked me for my honesty and paid me another six months' severance. I could now concentrate on Russia full time.

By this time I was traveling to Russia one week out of every five or six, and Bob was keeping an eye on my parents and their deteriorating health. This was shortly after the wall came down, and the Russian people were beginning to experience a new way of life. Capitalism and crime were on the rise. People were enjoying their newfound freedom and learning along the way. Back then, packing for a trip to Russia was unlike anything I had ever experienced even with all the traveling I had done up until that time. The first thing you put into your luggage was toilet paper. We normally stayed at the Radisson in downtown Moscow. Once you were inside the hotel you would have thought you were in a luxury hotel in any major city in America. Regardless, they didn't have toilet paper.

There were no rental cars. If you needed a car for an extended period of time, you needed to hire a private individual who had car. I doubt insurance existed back then, so God help us if we got into an auto accident, and it was amazing that we didn't, with the crazy driving habits of many of the local people. We needed to hire drivers with cars for each of the salesmen on the street. Initially there were only a few, but the numbers grew as business improved. When we visited the business from the United States, we would hire drivers who also doubled as armed bodyguards. I used to say it was probably reminiscent of being in the liquor business here in the United States during the roaring twenties and the days of Al Capone. Violence was very much a part of the Capone era of Prohibition in Chicago, and it was very much a part of the new freedoms the Russian people were experiencing.

The cultural differences, language barriers, and just day-to-day societal differences created challenges to doing business every day. One of the most disturbing situations we were confronted with early in the operation was when we determined that a key manager was stealing from us. Quite frankly we were afraid to contact local law enforcement, so we thought we would try to handle it in a low-key way. Just to get rid of the problem, we determined we would have to terminate his employment, and we paid him a sum of money, hoping he would go away quietly. Shortly after the incident, the local manager was found in the Russian office, tied by his wrists and ankles, suspended between two radiators with the gas valve in the open position. Back in the early nineties, everyone in Russia smoked, but luckily for us our cleaning person didn't. As she came to the office that morning, she smelled the gas, discovered the manager, and immediately shut off the gas and untied him. While this experience was shocking, to say the least, the dark side of Russia was offset by the bright side.

On one of my first visits, we happened to be going by Saint Petersburg Square, known as Palace Square. It is the central city square of Saint Petersburg and the former Russian Empire. It is the place where the Bloody Sunday massacre occurred—the precursor to the Russian Revolution. As we passed by, I noticed that the square had several musicians playing music. I asked our driver to pull over so we could walk over closer to the activity. The musicians were made up of several different horn players and a tuba player playing "The Star-Spangled Banner" for tips. As we stood in amazement, we looked at each other, and all of us had tears streaming down our faces. The experience was very moving, and I wish I could share that experience today with some of our Olympic athletes and students at our major universities who think it is OK to disrespect our flag.

Further evidence of how fast our culture was spreading was demonstrated later that week when we were at a beer promotion at one of the local bars, which was having a chugging contest. It goes without saying that the Russian beer was terrible, and the more we could get the locals to sample American beer, the more popular our beer became. Somehow, I got dragged into a chugging contest with a big, full-bearded Russian who must have outweighed me by at least one hundred pounds. One of our salesmen thought it would be great fun to have an American competing with a Russian for the main chugging event. Never one to back down, I graciously agreed. Did I mention that the event was being televised on local Moscow TV? We were each given huge mugs that I'm sure held more than twenty-four ounces, and the contest began.

I have never been much of a beer chugger, but I was doing pretty well against the big Russian. At one time I was actually ahead, when I began to think that it might not be such a good idea to beat him, so I consciously slowed down and let him beat me. I think it turned out to be the right decision, as we spent the next several hours with his group, laughing, drinking beer, and telling jokes.

The joke-telling session was especially bizarre because of the language barrier. We could speak no Russian, and some of the Russians could speak just a little English. When a punch line was delivered, there would be this pause with a blank look on the participants' faces until it sunk in, followed by an outburst of laughter. The people were wonderful, and it was pretty obvious that our political problems are between the governments and not the people.

As capitalism began to spread in the liquor industry, new bars were opening on a regular basis. One such bar was called Night Flight. Our salespeople were anxious to show us their new account. While I hate to use the overworked word "amazing," it surely aptly describes this facility. Our bodyguards explained that they would be leaving their guns in the car because there were metal detectors at the entrance of the bar to be certain there were no armed patrons. The facility was a huge three- or four-story building that appeared from the outside like a warehouse. This was not unusual in that most of the buildings in Russia looked like warehouses. When you entered, after passing security (remember, this was 1994), there was a huge oblong bar in the center of the room. While there were both male and female bartenders and servers, they skewed female. All were scantily attired and very attractive—and I use the word "scantily" loosely. If you were sitting at the bar and looked up over your head, you saw a complete circus high-wire act and trapeze act. Only this time, they weren't scantily attired; they were completely nude—both the men and the women.

Prostitution was also not policed. Ladies of the evening were usually well represented in the more popular bars. Out of curiosity, one night my partner and I entered into a conversation with one of the ladies. We were very surprised when she told us she spoke three languages and had a degree in mathematics. I'll never forget her words when she said, "I'm not a bad girl, just want to meet Western businessman and get out of this place. Russia not good, want to go to America."

As my trips to Moscow continued, I became aware of benefits not always known to an inexperienced Russian traveler like me. On one of my rides with one of the salesmen, we were in a market in the downtown Moscow. This particular market was an open-air poultry-and-meat shop. The meat and poultry were displayed hanging from the ceiling and in cabinets; most of it was not refrigerated. To my surprise there was a big barrel filled with caviar. While the lady working there told me it was beluga, I can't be sure, but it sure tasted like it. That day I was leaving to come back home, so I wanted to bring some back with me. The lady took an old-fashioned Ball jar, filled it with caviar, and put a piece of aluminum foil on the top with several rubber bands. She charged me six American dollars. I bought two additional sealed containers for about twelve dollars each, thinking that if the bulk didn't work out, at least I would have something to show for my effort.

When I got to the airport in Moscow, since there was no security, I simply got on the plane. When the flight attendant greeted me, I asked her if she liked caviar. When she replied that she did, I gave her one of the smaller containers and told her it was hers if she would put the rest of mine in the refrigerator until we got to New York. She did, and once I got to JFK, it was just matter of getting some ice from one of the bars and keeping it cold until I got home.

On my flight home, I began to think about the different brands of beer I had observed being sold in Moscow. While most were unknown brands, there were several popular European beers available also, including Heineken. Upon arriving back home, I contacted one of my old associates working for Heineken and inquired how they were getting their beer into the country. I told him we were in the beginning stages of setting up an American-style beer distributor there with Miller products. I asked whether there was any possibility that we could represent Heineken as well. He told me he didn't know but would inquire at their headquarters in Amsterdam.

Several days later, at some time in the early morning hours, my phone rang. This was obviously before caller ID; you had to answer the phone to determine who was calling. In my sleepy condition, I answered to a distinctly Belgian accent. The voice on the other end of the line spoke. "Hello, Tom, this is Franz with the Heineken brewery in Amsterdam. I apologize for the time, but there was simply no other way to contact you." When I realized who I was speaking with, I actually stood at attention next to my bed. As we talked, it soon became very clear that Franz was vice president of worldwide distribution. He said he would be interested in discussing our operation in Moscow in more detail at a later date. We scheduled a meeting in Amsterdam later in the month.

When the time came, I scheduled a flight from Moscow to Hamburg, Germany, and then boarded a train to Amsterdam. While I could have flown direct to Amsterdam, I chose this route to be able to explore other small German breweries to expand our product line even further. Breweries are most profitable when operating at full capacity. If our company could buy these small breweries' excess capacity, they would be more profitable and we would have more brands for sale—or so I thought.

It was a fun trip but ultimately produced few results. I miscalculated the ease of communicating. I found that English was not predominantly spoken, and the only German I knew was "*danke*." I did, however, sample more German brands of beer than probably most Germans do in a lifetime, and I had a pleasant glow all the way to Amsterdam.

As with any new undertaking, funding for our operation was, to say the least, scant. While I received a share of the company when I agreed to join the board, there was no salary associated with my travel and expenses. The partners kept a running total of our individual expenses to be reimbursed sometime in the future, when we hoped the company would be flush.

The potential Heineken involvement presented me with a unique opportunity. I created a contract with the partners that would pay me twenty-five cents for every case that was sold for the first ten years of operation if I was successful in bringing in the Heineken brands. Because of uncertainty surrounding the Russian government, we, the partners, and the Heineken management knew that a franchise agreement was out of the question. We all settled on a loosely written letter of commitment and intent that I drafted in the Heineken offices in Amsterdam.

Now we just had to raise enough money to get the operation off the ground. Needless to say, it was hard to contain my excitement as the days moved on. Next step was a board meeting to raise the additional capital. The journey continued again, with more detours.

While I was in Amsterdam, the partners were busy at home trying to raise the needed capital. We were pretty much tapped out. I had invested around 150 grand, and the three other partners made considerably larger investments. The additional money would have to come from the outside, and with it reduced ownership for the original partners.

As luck would have it, one of the partners had been talking about our company to a friend and neighbor who had just sold a business he had inherited from his dad and was cash rich. He was invited to our capital-raising meeting and agreed to invest half a million dollars, making him the second-largest investor.

All the pieces on the chess board were beginning to fall in place. Months earlier we had hired a young man from New Jersey whose family had interests in Russia. In a very short time, he was able to figure out how the navigate Russian politics and the Russian mafia. The next several months were the first in a long time where we could see progress being made. Beer was being ordered, beer was being sold, and we were slowly beginning to see light at the end of the tunnel. It appeared to be the perfect time for another board meeting.

We set up a time for the business meeting so that we could bring in our New Jersey wonder boy. He gave a complete presentation on how business was now being done in Russia. The presentation included a complete description of who along the chain of distribution, from customs at the ships' receiving dock to the end consumer, was on the take. The number of people along the way that had to be paid off was considerable, but we were still able to pay the bribes and sell beer at a profit.

By now we were able to figure out the steps needed to sell beer in Russia for rubles, transfer the money to Canada, convert it to US dollars, and transfer it to our bank in Tampa, Florida. We now could see we were really making progress, or so we thought.

That progress was short lived: our newest stockholder said he refused to be involved with a company that was breaking US security law. We would be prohibited from taking the company public in the future. I sat in the meeting and reached a slow boil. This was not a company that could be taken public to begin with. We had developed a cash cow. It would continue to be so until the bribes got out of hand or the government changed its mind. This company would generate huge amounts of cash for the partners. When it was over, we would shut it down, take our respective share of the profits, and move on. Heineken, a company experienced in doing business in many different countries with different rules and customs, had no problem with what we were doing. They were concerned with one thing: selling beer and getting paid for it. We should be too.

I couldn't believe the stupidity, but he was insistent, convincing the other two major stockholders to vote with him. After I'd spent a year of my time on this, it was obvious to me that everything we worked for was going up in smoke. I sat back in my chair and said, "If you are actually serious, we will be bankrupt by the end of the year." The prospects for my twenty-five-cents-per-case commission that would set me up for life were now looking pretty grim.

Our office was in Tampa, and over the next months, we continued to operate within the new guidelines established by the new money guy. My mom had died in the interim, and I had moved my dad into assisted living. I still had my apartment in downtown Chicago. I told Bob he could live in my parents' house until it was sold, and then he would have to find something else.

Bob

GUT PUNCH

Since I was splitting my time between Chicago and Florida, I decided to move the boat to Chicago. The weekend in question presented us with a questionable weather forecast. We decided to take a chance but were forced to seek shelter in Racine, Wisconsin, because of weather. I went back to Chicago while Bob stayed on the boat.

A couple of days later, he called and told me he'd met a guy on the dock delivering a boat from Florida, complaining about having to deadhead back to Florida. He said the guy asked him if he knew anyone who might be interested in shipping a boat to Florida. Once again, operating under the assumption that God works in strange ways, *High Life* and Bob were on their way to Clearwater, Florida. I would use the boat for my residence when in Florida, and Bob was now near the VA Hospital in Saint Petersburg, still living rent-free for what was now going on two years.

I learned over time that Bob was a very interesting character. Because of his war injuries, he spent many hours in the dayroom while convalescing in the hospital. The room was set up for patients to be able to see outside and feel the warmth of the sun shining through the windows. As he described it to me, there was also an upright piano in the room. He told me he would have the aides position his bed so that he could lie on his stomach and would be above the keyboard. He would spend hours in the dayroom plunking around on the piano until he taught himself to play. If I hadn't seen and heard it for myself, I wouldn't have believed it. One of the bars we used to frequent in Clearwater, Florida, had a stand-up piano. Periodically he would do an improv honky-tonk piano solo, and people would buy him beers. The owners offered him a job, but Bob avoided any stress associated with responsibility. In Bob's mind he had his hands full taking care of the *High Life*, the sailboat.

I continued to split my time between Florida and Chicago, with more and more time being spent in Clearwater, on the boat. I was also trying to get in a few trips to Colorado to satisfy my snow-skiing fix at the time. By this time Carol and I had had our first date. I had told Carol about the time I was spending in Florida and asked her if she would like to come for a weekend of sailing. She told me that she had a conference coming up in Fort Lauderdale and maybe we could coordinate our schedules around her upcoming trip to Florida. I gave Carol the phone number of the boat and told her that I would be in Florida the same time as her conference. I told her to call me at the conclusion of the conference and we would get together in Clearwater. Bob and I spent available time cleaning and getting the boat presentable. The weekend passed with no call.

CHAPTER 19

REFLECTIONS ON ROMANCE

While I was deeply disappointed, I was not discouraged. From my own experience, I knew that for active people with active schedules, things come up that are unavoidable, and I hoped that was the case with Carol. Gambling that there had simply been a breakdown in communication, I called Carol at work the following week. I told her I would have a prepaid airline ticket to Tampa waiting for her if she wanted to come for a sailing weekend. It ultimately worked out, and she came for the weekend. We would learn many months later that she actually had called and left a message on the answering machine on the boat. Bob had forgotten to tell me.

We continued to see each other and talked regularly on the phone until she returned to Florida for the Thanksgiving weekend in the fall of 1995. We celebrated the holiday, and she prepared a complete Thanksgiving dinner in the galley of the sailboat while I roasted a turkey on a Weber grill on the dock. Carol made mashed potatoes, dressing, cranberries, and all the trimmings while sitting on the dock enjoying the weather and my boat.

As I sit here and reflect on the moment, I'm sure it was the best Thanksgiving ever. In all my previous relationships, I never had anyone that shared my interests. I had finally found someone who loved sailing and snow skiing as much as I did: a match truly made in heaven. To us, it was more than a cliché. Carol's dad, Blackie, had died when she was in her early twenties, and my mom had recently died. We shared the experience of each having a parent who wanted to see their kid happy but for some reason had been unable to find happiness for themselves. We joked many times that we were certain Blackie and Viola, my mom, were involved somehow.

The year was coming to an end, but our relationship was just beginning. I still had at least one more Russia trip to complete, but I was pretty sure it would be the last. Just one more trip to satisfy the caviar habit. I could have bought a lot more caviar with the money I had already invested, but the experience was priceless.

We spent much of the Thanksgiving weekend getting to know each other, and it became very obvious that a trip to Vail over the Christmas holiday needed to be scheduled. When my condo partner, Ed, and I had bought the condo, we made an agreement that because he had a family and I was single, he would get the Christmas weekend, and I would get New Year's. One of my condo neighbors owned a very popular steak house in Memphis. When he found out that I was in the beer business, we began a New Year's tradition of throwing a New Year's bash. He provided the food, including traditional Southern dishes like black-eyed peas, and I provided the beer.

By the time Carol and I were planning our first trip to Vail together, I had already owned the condo with Ed for over ten years. As a result, most of my friends were locals: ski instructors, bartenders, waitresses, and shopkeepers. My first trip to Vail was back when I was still living in California, when Ed called me and told me that he and his partner had just bought Vail Associates, the company that developed the ski area. He invited me to come to Vail over the Christmas holidays. I accepted by saying, "Thanks for the invite; I think the cost of my favorite sport has just been reduced significantly." From that point on, I saved my vacation days so I could use them all during the ski season in Vail every year.

Carol and I spent our first Christmas together in Vail. Since she was as avid a skier as I, we had a great time. Finally, someone with whom I could share my favorite pastime. I was able to smuggle in the last of my supply of caviar, and we put it to use in our New Year's celebration. We did not share it with the neighbor serving black-eyed peas and herring. Carol had never had caviar before, so I had prepared the toast points and crème fraîche and put out the crushed-ice container and the mother-of-pearl serving pieces along with the champagne. With all the cheap caviar I had brought back from Russia over the past two years, I had become quite the connoisseur. When I came back from taking my shower, I found Carol eating the caviar like she would Ruffles and French onion dip. "You don't need all that fancy stuff," she said. "Just dip it like you would chips and dip." The more time I spent with her, the more I knew she was the one for me.

CHAPTER 20

REFLECTIONS ON IMPORTANT DECISIONS

As vice president of sales for Miller, I worked closely with our director of finance, Chris Grant. He walked into my office at Miller one morning and told me he was resigning. He was starting his own investment advisory management business and would be looking for clients. I was sorry to see him leave Miller because he was very good at his job. He was a graduate of Wharton business school. At the time I did not have much of a portfolio, but nonetheless I became his first client. Later, after being forced to resign, my golden parachute was significant and allowed me a little freedom in pursuing other interests.

Our Russian operation went into bankruptcy before the end of the year, as I predicted. It was taken over by Heineken and operated quite successfully, with the same local guy from New Jersey running the show just as he had asked us to do.

On one of my last trips back from Moscow, I remember calling Chris from a bar in Manhattan. The stock market had once again had a record day. I had made as much money that week as I had at Miller in a year. As we talked, it became apparent that I should have listened to him when, before I went to Russia, he was trying to convince me to get my securities license. As a matter of fact, he had given me the textbook so I could study for the tests on the long flights to Russia and back.

At the conclusion of our phone call, it was obvious to me that a career in the financial industry might be my next journey. And so it was that I dusted off the books he had given me and took the first step on the next journey: getting my securities license. Once again, at the age of about forty-eight, I would be reinventing myself.

Studying for the various licenses was very difficult for me, but nonetheless I persevered, and by 2001 I had passed all the tests, including the most important, Series 7, which was the granddaddy of securities tests. From a low of 3,600 in late 1994, the Dow soared 36 percent in the next year. The birth of the internet led to new efficiencies in communication and commerce by the end of the 1990s. No one believed it, but by July 1996, the Dow was over 5,500, and by April of 1998, it had surpassed 9,000. As I sit here today in the year 2021, it is hard to believe we are at over 35,000 today. I was living the old adage of "I'd rather be lucky than smart," but I'd like to think my success was a combination of both.

Chris and I had initially talked about starting our own firm after I'd passed the tests, but much like in the real estate business, you need to hang your license with a recognized broker-dealer. I hung my license with his firm temporarily until we could figure out next steps. Could we be successful in attracting new clients, clients who trusted us enough to give us serious money to manage for them? It was obvious from the beginning that people were not going to give their serious money to a beer salesman. However, because Chris had an impressive track record with me and my portfolio, we felt we had a story to tell that was compelling.

The first test came at one of my annual hunting trips to South Dakota the year I got my securities license. I had been hunting in South Dakota since my first assignment there back in 1972. Over the years, the local distributor and I developed an annual outing. In 1992 the governor started what he called the Governor's Hunt, where businessmen from around the country were invited to participate. It was the governor's hope that it would entice businesses to come to South Dakota. The Miller distributor in Sioux Falls arranged for me to be invited. The following year the governor suspended the hunt, but our Miller distributor continued the tradition, only this time we would invite other beer distributors from around the country that shared our interest in pheasant hunting.

It had been about six years since I left Miller and about two or three since I had been working with Heileman and the Russia venture. And so it was that when Jim Burma, the distributor from Sioux Falls, asked the question in front of all the other guys at our evening cocktail party—"So, Koehler, what are you doing for money these days, since you're unemployed again?"—I responded that I was in the process of starting a money-management firm and wanted him for one of our first clients. In response he looked around the group and said, "Why don't we have our cocktail party in my room tomorrow night and let Koehler explain why we should let him manage our money?"

And so the next night, about a dozen guys crammed into a bedroom at the Holiday Inn Express in Mitchell, South Dakota, and listened to me explain our investment strategy. One of the most significant elements of the strategy was the use of options to generate extra cash flow. Most important, my partner and I were invested in the same companies and investment instruments that we were putting our clients in. I asked my audience, "Has your broker invested his own money as well?"

My pitch must have been effective, because before we adjourned to the bar, two of the distributors told me to come visit their offices. Jim was one of those interested and told me he wanted to be one of my first clients. He told me that he had trusted my judgment when I was with Miller and became very rich. And so Grant Koehler & Levin LTD was born in the Holiday Inn Express, in a room with two double beds and a dozen guys sitting around drinking beer and scotch.

During the same time, my relationship with Carol continue to grow. She had a very demanding career and spent a lot of time traveling, mostly to New York. I continued to travel back and forth between Chicago and Clearwater, Florida. With my dad in a nursing home, I knew he had better care than I could provide, but I still wanted to see him as much as possible.

If anything good came from my experience in Russia other than cheap caviar, it was that I realized that at this point in my life I wanted to live in a warm climate. I decided I would find a house and hopefully move my dad to Florida as well. In the back of my mind, I was also hoping that moving to Florida was something Carol would consider as well. Between Carol's travel schedule and our mutual desire to spend time in the mountains of Colorado and on the boat in Florida, we had a very full schedule. I knew that I was falling in love with Carol, and I was pretty sure the feeling was mutual. This became even more apparent when one evening she jokingly said she didn't believe in long engagements, and we weren't even engaged yet. A friend of hers was in the jewelry business, and one day I called him and swore him to silence but asked him whether he would help me design an engagement ring for Carol. Since my mother had recently died, I wanted to use some of the diamonds from both her ring and my grandmother's.

CHAPTER 21

REFLECTIONS ON THE HAPPIEST DAY OF MY LIFE

Roughly a year after Carol and I started dating, on her birthday in September 1996, I asked her to marry me, and lucky me, she accepted. Talk about new journeys. As I write this, I'm starting to realize just how many I've been on. My priority list was simple: get married, successfully start a new business, and move to Florida. While Carol had a good job and we didn't want to lose the income, we still didn't know if she could work remotely from Colorado and Florida or whether her company would require she still work out of her office in Chicago. Throughout our engagement and early stages of our marriage, we learned how to juggle pretty well and keep all the balls in the air. We knew, however, that we couldn't do it long term.

During one of our many trips to Florida, I was contacted by my real estate broker and advised that she had found a home that she thought Carol and I would enjoy. It was in Clearwater Beach, on the water and off the Intracoastal Waterway. It had a deepwater dock for the sailboat and a covered boathouse and a lift for a second, smaller boat. It also had a guest dock for visiting boaters and was five minutes from the Gulf of Mexico. It sounded perfect! The broker advised me that we needed to see the property right away because it had just come on the market and would not be available long.

I had been cleaning the dock box at the time of her call and told her that while we would be happy to view the house, I was pretty grubby at the time and didn't smell too good either. She said she was more worried that the house would not stay on the market long than she was worried about how I looked and smelled. We went to see the house in the next hour and made an offer by the end of the day.

OUR FIRST HOUSE IN CLEARWATER FLORIDA

Since the house had been built in the late seventies, it needed considerable updating. The kitchen needed new cabinets, countertops, backsplashes, and appliances. Painting and new carpets were also necessary. The house had two master suites. One was downstairs and the other was upstairs, directly over the downstairs suite, with the same floor plan. My plan was to move my dad in from the nursing home. I was hoping to engage a full-time caregiver and move Dad into the house in Florida when it was complete.

By now I had moved out of my apartment in Chicago and was splitting my time between Carol's house in Des Plaines, the boat in Florida, and now the new house in Clearwater Beach. Slowly Carol would spend more and more weekends with me, supervising the work on the house and shopping for furniture. It became a routine. On Friday I would pick up Carol and

GUT PUNCH

her cat, Casper, at the Tampa airport, and I'd drop them off on Sunday night or Monday morning so she could return to work. Not sure how many frequent-flier miles Casper accumulated, but I'm sure he would have qualified for a free ticket if the airlines had a category for cats.

As we neared completion, we spent more and more time in Florida, until one morning I received a call from the nursing home advising me that my father had died in his sleep. It is hard to lose a family member. Since my mother died, my dad's dementia condition had continued to deteriorate. When I visited, he would usually remember me, but he would always ask why my mom wasn't coming to visit. It used to tear my heart out to have to retell the story of Mom's passing. The good news is that he went quietly in his sleep and is now with the love of his life.

MARCH 22, 1997

I proposed to Carol on her birthday, September 13, 1996, and in keeping with her belief in short engagements, we planned our wedding for March 1997. Since we met in Vail, Colorado, we decided that Vail was a perfect location to get married. We figured that we would invite only our closest friends and relatives and only the truly closest ones would invest the time and money to get to a Rocky Mountain wedding. In the end sixty-five people responded affirmatively.

The event began with an on-mountain reception and rehearsal dinner at Beano's Cabin, an award-winning restaurant nestled in a mountain meadow at the base of Larkspur Bowl at an elevation of just under ten thousand feet. It is accessible only by one-hour horseback ride or a diesel John Deere tractor in the spring and summer or by a beautiful horse-drawn sleigh in the winter. We had several sleighs for the excursion up the mountain. Once everyone was settled in their seats, the attendant distributed blankets so everyone would remain warm and comfy. As we slowly left the base of Beaver Creek and ventured up the mountain, the artificial light was gradually replaced by the bright moonlight. This, plus the quiet of the forest punctuated by the sleigh bells on the horses, was all that was needed to create a magical, almost surreal, adventure.

Champagne brunch after the morning church service

When we arrived at our destination, we were welcomed by an elegant rustic cabin featuring a vaulted ceiling, antler chandeliers, and a large stone hearth and fireplace with a wraparound deck and stunning views. The moon appeared so close that you felt you could simply reach out and touch it. The evening featured a local vocalist/guitarist, giving new meaning to the term "Rocky Mountain High." John Denver would have been proud.

My Beautiful Bride

The Chapel at Beaver Creek

Beano's Cabin prides itself on its outstanding service and extensive wine list with a menu that features a variety of local favorites. We knew it would be an experience our friends would not soon forget. Nor would we. The surprise of the evening was that—unbeknownst to me—the Miller Brewing Company had reserved the other half of the restaurant for the winners of an incentive contest, and I knew many of the people there.

Our Friends Enjoying the Day

GUT PUNCH

RECEPTION AT SADDLE RIDGE

The Friday-night reception was followed by a service at the Beaver Creek Chapel at nine the next morning. One of my local friends was quick to comment, "You would think a beer salesman would know better than to have a church service so early in the morning after a night of partying on the mountain." Loud enough for everyone to hear, it set the stage for the service that would follow. The morning was spectacular, with powder blue skies and wispy puffs of white clouds dancing on the mountaintop.

The service was followed by a champagne breakfast featuring alpenhorn players and accordion players to provide an authentic Austrian Alps atmosphere for the day to come. As we finished our champagne breakfast and headed to the chairlift, you could hear German and Austrian music being played in the background, once again amplifying the atmosphere that the Vail Valley is known for. Each respondent was given a complimentary ski pass for a day of skiing. We were somewhat worried about the liability associated with providing lift tickets for our guests without obtaining the usual waiver of liability from each of them. The ski-hill liability is automatically waived when you purchase your lift ticket, or you don't get the ticket. In essence, I gave the hill the waiver when I purchased the tickets, but by giving them to our guests, we were assuming the liability.

The biggest challenge associated with the complimentary lift tickets came from Carol's seventy-year-old aunt, who decided on Friday night that she wanted to learn how to ski. After considerable dialogue and pleading, plus plying her with copious amounts of vodka, we were able to convince her that learning to ski at the age of seventy was probably not the smartest idea.

Luckily there were no accidents, and all our guests made it to the reception at Saddle Ridge for an evening of dinner and dancing. Our special day was truly a fairy-tale wedding and one of the most memorable days of my life.

By this time, we had sold Carol's house in Des Plaines, Illinois. We remained in Vail after the wedding until the end of the ski season, and then returned to Clearwater. Carol had received permission from her company to work remotely from both our locations. Shortly after returning to Florida, we picked up the next addition to our family. She was a purebred Lab and stole our hearts from the day we brought her home as a puppy. We named her Cheyenne, and she traveled with us everywhere.

Ten months later we were faced with our first tragedy. Because Carol was still very active in her business, we still spent much time apart. We would try to spend our free time together, catching up on things that occurred when we were apart. Walking Cheyenne provided the opportunity to do that. One particular morning, while we were walking and talking, we learned a valuable leash lesson. Our routine usually allowed us to walk her for a portion without her leash and then leash her when we got to an area with more traffic. This morning, however, our dialogue was interrupted by screeching tires and yelping cries from our precious Cheyenne. She had been hit by a passing pickup truck.

GUT PUNCH

For the next twelve weeks, we nursed our baby back to health as she went through several surgeries and extensive recuperation. Spending as much time as we did in both Vail and Florida, we soon learned that we would need cars in both locations. Renting a car for the time we spent in Vail was more costly than buying one and leaving it there.

Eventually we would settle into a routine where we left for Vail right after spending Thanksgiving with Carol's mom in Chicago. We would stay for the ski season and then usually return to Florida in mid- to late April. After hearing horror stories about the airlines from a close friend who was a flight attendant, we became concerned about Cheyenne's safety and began driving back and forth three or four times a year.

The High Life

Because of the time that Carol and I were spending in Vail, there came a point when my business partner, Ed, and I decided it was time to sell the Beaver Creek condo, probably one of my better investments. Carol and I took the profits and bought a townhome in Wildridge. It was located in Avon, looking down on Beaver Creek; we gave up the ski-in, ski-out convenience for more space and privacy.

For the next several years, we split our time between Vail in the winter and Clearwater in the summer. By this time, I had totally restored the 1972 Gulfstar sloop inside and out, and we were ready for some serious Florida cruising. We cruised the Intracoastal Waterway and the Gulf of Mexico from Clearwater Beach to the Naples / Marco Island area. We soon learned we had the wrong boat for the type of cruising we were doing. First, we had a five-foot keel beneath the hull of our boat. The Gulf of Mexico is very shallow, and the ICW has some shallow spots as well. In a very short period of time, I think we ran aground on most of them. The second thing we learned was that Florida summer, especially in August and September, is very hot. It took us only a few trips to become jealous of the motor cruisers who would cruise by us in their air-conditioned cabins, sipping their cocktails. As hard as it was, I eventually sold my pride and joy and bought a forty-foot Carver cruiser.

The Diva First cruise to Captiva Island

CHAPTER 22

REFLECTING ON THE VISION OF OUR OWN FIRM

As I have discussed before, by November of 1999 I had passed the relevant SEC requirements I needed to be able to start our own firm. On the morning of September 11, 2001, I was on the phone from our townhome in Colorado discussing the potential buyout of Chris's current partner. I had the TV on in my office, and while his partner was trying to make some minor changes to the offer we were discussing, I observed the planes flying into the World Trade Center. I asked them if they had their TV on, to which they replied they did not. I told them to turn on their TV and we should check in with each other later in the day. Since he had not accepted our offer as submitted, I was withdrawing it. Who knew if or when the stock market would open.

September 11 made us rethink the location of our primary residence. We found that we were spending more and more time in Colorado. We decided that maybe it was time for us to relocate to Colorado. Since we had decided not to buy out Chris's existing partner, we were now able to move forward with the steps necessary to start our own firm on a smaller scale. While we started out small, we were ultimately able to build our business to over 250 clients.

Prior to 9/11, we had made plans to attend the Winter Olympics in Salt Lake City but put those plans on hold after the attack. As we got closer to February, we began to warm up to the idea and began to think that rather than being dangerous, it was probably the safest place in America. Because of my local Vail connection to the US ski team, we were able to get tickets to the opening ceremony. As expected, security was extremely tight. We went through several checkpoints before getting to our seats. At one such checkpoint we were searched. Before leaving home, I had transferred some very expensive cognac to a flask I usually carried for those especially cold days on the ski hills of Vail, never thinking that it would be an issue sitting in the stands at the opening ceremony. Wrong. When the security guards discovered my flask, they gave me a choice: either drink it before entering or dump it. They had no problem with the flask itself, just the contents. Unwilling to get totally drunk drinking the contents of my flask and probably passing out during the ceremony and being unable to remember any of it, I summoned my friends to the rescue. We all took a healthy hit from the flask. I offered the guards the opportunity to share, which they politely declined as they poured out the rest of the cognac in a snowbank. Our bodies responded to the warm wave passing from lips to tummy just enough to warm us up for the cold evening that would follow.

While security was definitely enhanced, it was not obtrusive. Once seated, we could hear the helicopters above us and the F-16 at higher altitudes. Ever since that first experience at the county fair that I described earlier, where I cried at the playing of the national anthem, I have always been moved by patriotic events. While I usually cry at the drop of a hat when I am observing the flag and the troops, there are three events that will remain vividly burned in my mind, the first two being the county fair when I was a child and the Saint Petersburg Square on one of my trips to Russia. Now this, the third: the 2002 Olympic opening ceremony in Salt Lake City, Utah.

You had come to expect the procession of countries if you ever watched other opening day ceremonies. This one, however, took an unexpected turn that struck an emotional chord with everyone in the audience. It was so moving that as I sit here trying to convey the images properly and accurately as I recall them, I am once again moved to tears. But maybe that's just me. Shortly before the American athletes entered the arena, in seats below where we were seated, we were able to observe President George W. Bush, accompanied by his Secret Service detail, ushered to his seats.

PRESENTATION OF THE COLORS AT THE OPENING
CEREMONIES OF THE 2002 WINTER OLYMPICS

Before the athletes entered, the lights were turned down and the stadium was completely quiet. The torn flag from ground zero was carried into the stadium by an honor guard made up of American athletes, firefighters, and police. All you could hear was the cadence count by the honor guard leader: "Hup, hup, hup." Complete silence while the helicopters hovered over the stadium and the F-16 did flyovers at lower altitudes.

As the flag was displayed, a spotlight moved from the flag to an individual at the very top of the stadium. Since our seats were high up, we were able to get a good view. Standing near the top of the stadium was a Native American from Utah who was a bird handler. On his arm was a bald eagle, which he subsequently released. On its way down to another handler at the base of the stadium, the eagle soared past us, so close that you felt you could reach out and touch it. It soared over the crowd, coming so close to the president you would have thought it was going to land on his shoulder. The eagle eventually connected with the other handler. At the very end, the spotlight moved to focus on President Bush, where he made a cell phone call to one of our Olympic skaters as the athletes entered the stadium.

By this time, as you can imagine, I was crying uncontrollably. Somewhat embarrassed by my emotional breakdown, I looked over at my friends to see that I was not alone in my tears. We all had tear-streaked cheeks and were breaking into smiles. It is heartbreaking to see the patriotic decay that has infiltrated our culture in the past twenty years. Parents, teachers, and our politicians should be ashamed for the role they have played. God help our country!

CHAPTER 23

REALITY—SEPTEMBER 2021: THE WAIT CONTINUES

Carol's birthday, and we are still waiting. No one's fault; that's just how it is. My urologist wanted to do another PSA test before we made any major decisions. He wanted to wait at least thirty days. The results came in last week, and they were higher than the previous test thirty days ago. We are now in the process of scheduling a biopsy of the prostate. Not something I'm looking forward to, but it needs to be done before they can recommend treatment. Prostate problems are very common among men my age. A very good friend of mine was diagnosed with prostate cancer at the age of fifty. He is my age now and cancer-free. I can only hope for similar results.

Once again, however, a cloud over what should otherwise be a celebration for Carol. Tonight, we will try to put it behind us. We plan to have dinner with our dear friends Jim and Nancy at the Palm Beach Yacht Club.

About ten days later, September 24, 1:00 p.m., Dr. Rodin, my urologist, sits across from me in the examining room and starts out by saying, "I have some good news and bad news. What would you like first? Let's start out with the bad news because even the bad news isn't so bad." The bad news is that they found cancer in one of the twelve locations that they biopsied. The good news is that it is rated at the very lowest of the scale used to quantify prostate cancer. The next steps are simply waiting six months for another PSA test and most likely another biopsy in a year.

It's hard to stay positive when the bad news keeps piling up. Life is in constant motion. Even when you think you know what's going to happen, something completely different takes center stage.

When Chris and I started our business, one of our first clients was an associate of mine from back when I worked in Southern California. We'll call him Mr. Mike. Mr. Mike was very active in managing his own portfolio and loved doing it. When Mr. Mike came to us as a client, he had suffered several large losses and was very cautious. He had recently retired and needed his serious money to grow. When I knew Mr. Mike in LA, he was a player and lived in the fast lane. Once he retired, his lifestyle calmed down. He was an avid kayaker and would spend hours on the Intracoastal Waterway. He was in excellent physical shape and lived within his means. Once or twice a year, he would vacation abroad with buddies. Together, we were able to rebuild his portfolio into a sizable multimillion-dollar holding.

About two years before my cancer diagnosis, I received a call from Mr. Mike requesting a meeting. I met with him and his neighbor and learned that recently he had been having some health problems, primarily with sight and memory. At this time Mr. Mike had not yet reached seventy years of age. I learned of phone calls in the middle of the night and requests to help read his mail. As a result of the meeting, I recognized the burden that he had unintentionally put on his neighbor was unfair to the neighbor and some changes would need to be made. He would need the help of a caregiver. I was instrumental in getting him a lawyer, and his neighbor introduced him to a caregiver agency.

We began to try to get his life in order. We created a living will and a trust. Mr. Mike appointed me trustee should his condition progress to the point he was unable to make decisions for himself. He told me that I was the only one in his life that he trusted with the responsibility.

Mr. Mike went through several caregivers, and one day he brought his latest to Carol's and my house to visit. While Carol gave the caregiver a tour of our house, Mr. Mike indicated he wanted to pay the caregiver under the table in addition to what he was paying the agency. I told him we would discuss it privately in the future and that we would make that decision after we had a track record to judge the quality of care. He agreed that it was early in the relationship and it was wise to wait. After several months we did eventually pay her another $1,000 monthly.

Later, after they left, Carol asked me, "Do you think it was strange that the first thing she said to me was 'Don't worry, I'm not going to marry Mr. Mike'?" I discovered that early in her assignment to help Mr. Mike, he had her doing things on his computer to help him continue his interest in the stock market. I am guessing, but I'm sure early on she saw the number of zeros in front of the decimal point, and her imagination started working overtime.

I could tell over time, as Mr. Mike's condition declined, that there was a relationship building. At a subsequent meeting with the lawyer, I had obtained for Mr. Mike, she approached me and asked who should she talk to in order to be put in Mr. Mike's will. I told her that was myself, and I didn't see that happening any time soon.

As Mr. Mike's condition continued to deteriorate, I felt that she was manipulating Mr. Mike. I had to walk a fine line to protect Mr. Mike yet not upset him regarding the personal feeling she was trying to exploit.

While the caregiver in question was the lead person on the team, there were other caregivers assigned to him as well. Mr. Mike had a beautiful condo on the Intracoastal Waterway. One night when he was being looked after by another member of the team, he got confused and walked outside, looking for the caregiver he had become attached to. Because he was unsupervised and his sight was failing rapidly, he ended up falling into the Intracoastal Waterway and was ultimately rescued by the local fire department.

I got the call from the hospital. As a result, I was summoned by Florida's social welfare agency. Together with the caregiver agency, we needed to convince the agent that we would take the necessary steps to ensure Mr. Mike's safety. While the accident was serious, in some ways it was a blessing in disguise in that it allowed us to terminate the problem caregiver. For the next several months, we rotated through several different caregivers. At one point we decided to move Mr. Mike into an assisted living facility. While we were encouraged by the two caregivers we finally found, we were certain that a facility would be better for Mr. Mike.

And then came COVID. The facility wouldn't accept Mr. Mike. In the end it worked out better in that the new caregivers were two sisters, and they treated Mr. Mike like he was a member of their family.

During the COVID shutdown, Mr. Mike's condition continued to worsen. He is now confined exclusively to his bed. He is conscious for brief moments when he is fed or given water. Sometimes he may smile when we talk to him, but it is unlikely that he comprehends anything. The caregivers feed him, give him water at scheduled intervals, and change his diapers. This is the life of what was once a vibrant man with the financial resources to live a very fulfilling life.

When he originally asked me to be his trustee, he requested that he be allowed to stay in his condo for as long as possible. If it became unsafe for him or he was financially unable to continue the private care, he would consider a care facility. Speaking candidly, if we moved him to a facility right now, I don't think he would know the difference. In my mind, a promise is a promise, and we will try to keep him in his condo for as long as we can. The caregivers we have now provide better care than he would receive in a facility. They refer to him as Papa.

By now you have probably figured out why I chose to include this story in this part of my journey. When faced with the fight against cancer, it is very easy to feel sorry for oneself. While I try to be positive and cherish every day, some days it's not always possible. During the last two years, as I was on my journey, I observed Mr. Mike go from a vibrant, mature man ready to enjoy his retirement to a vegetable, although still able to smile. We're just not sure he knows he's smiling.

The future comes whether you're ready or not. We all know death is inevitable, but when you know that your timetable may be sooner than you thought, it is very easy to become depressed. Comparing my life to Mr. Mike's helps keeps me from destructive depression. Fear does not stop death; it stops life. Worrying does not take away tomorrow's troubles; it takes away today's peace. These beliefs are what gets me through every day. I don't know what I would do without Carol and Savannah. I feel so blessed to have them and feel sorry for all the people out there who must face cancer alone.

CHAPTER 24

REFLECTIONS ON MORE CHANGES

As I mentioned earlier, the whole terrorism thing caused us to rethink our decision to make Florida our permanent residence. The news reports that the 9/11 pilots were trained at a flight school in Florida helped us decide that perhaps it was time to move to the mountains. After all, snow skiing was our first love, and why not take advantage of the opportunity while we were young enough to enjoy it? We were uncertain how long it would take to sell our Florida house but decided to put it on the market and test the water. We received a full offer in less than a month.

We weren't ready to give up our Florida location, because the boating interest was still strong. The plan was to just flip-flop the location of our permanent residence. We would maintain a smaller residence in Florida while the place we would call home would be Colorado.

By this time, we had sold the condo in Beaver Creek and settled into a townhome in Wildridge, a skiing community, overlooking Beaver Creek Mountain. It was about a fifteen-minute ride to the ski areas. We decided to build instead of buy and began the process. At the same time, we decided that while we enjoyed the west coast of Florida, it was time for a change. Carol had explored various east coast areas and settled on a new community in Palm City, Florida, located about thirty miles north of Palm Beach. It was a combination golf and yacht club that provided slip space for my boat and easy access to the Atlantic Ocean. Never to be accused of doing things the easy way, we began the undertaking of building two houses at the same time. So I moved the boat into the yet-to-be-completed marina in Palm Cove, and we got started. The good news was that it would take over three years before the developer was able to turn the community over to the residents, and I was able to keep my boat in the marina free of charge for three years.

The building experiences were very different. Once we decided on the location and purchased the lot, we met with the builder in Colorado and designed the house. I remember going over the plans at our kitchen table in Wildridge. When we completed the review, he looked up at me and said, "Well, Tom, what do you think? Do you want to build this?" I responded affirmatively, and he extended his hand across the table. We shook hands on it, and that was it. It was several months later, and well into the build, that we finally had contracts and signatures. I trusted him and he trusted me. Wow, what a concept.

At about the same time, we were starting the building process in Florida. We had picked out the model and selected a lot. What we thought would be a simple process—at least compared to building a house at nine-thousand-foot elevation—turned out to be a nightmare. When we sat down with the developer, after the basic floor plan was decided, everything was an add-on.

GUT PUNCH

At one point I joked that there was an upgrade fee for selecting electric lights over candles. Ironically, at the same time Carol and I were making these selections, I got a call from my new Colorado neighbor advising us that they had just moved the heavy equipment on our property to begin the excavation.

The Colorado home will always be our dream house and the best house we ever had. From groundbreaking to completion, the house was finished and move-in ready in eleven months. Quite unbelievable at an elevation of about nine thousand feet.

For the next six years, Vail was home. We would pack up the Suburban with Cheyenne in her kennel and make the thirty-six-hour trek four times a year. We would usually take off from Florida before Thanksgiving and spend the Thanksgiving weekend in Chicago with Carol's mother, then head to Vail, staying through spring skiing in April. Then it would be back to the warm Florida weather to take advantage of the great boating weather before hurricane season. Then back to Vail for hurricane season, and then start the routine all over again.

DRESS-UP DAY ON VAIL MOUNTAIN

We truly enjoyed being Vail locals. We made many friends and could experience the other great activities that the locale offered: horseback riding, hiking, snowshoeing, and even rafting. We even participated in a formal ski day where participants dressed in tuxedos and other formal attire. We loved every minute of our time in Vail and will always cherish our memories there.

Living in the mountains is not without its challenges, though. At the time we were there, many of the services we required on a regular basis were located in Denver, including service for our car, Carol's periodontist and urologist, some specialized medical care, and Costco. Naturally, the ninety-four-mile drive back to Denver was not without its weather challenges. Snowstorms are welcome when you need the snow to ski on, but they are not welcome when commuting back and forth to Denver and the pass is closed. Living in Vail is much easier and more fun when you are forty or fifty and not as much fun as you get older.

After a while the warm weather continued to draw us more strongly back to Florida. I remember sitting in my office in our home in Colorado, shortly after arriving from one of our thirty-six-hour trips, and asking Carol, "Honey, how long do you think we will want to do this? I think I'd rather be on my boat in Florida."

CHAPTER 25

REFLECTIONS ON EVEN MORE CHANGES

One of the hardest things we encountered while living in Colorado was watching the weather channel and the annual hurricanes threatening Florida. You felt so helpless knowing there was nothing you could do. Yes, you had insurance. But even that was uncertain: What if your insurance company went broke because of the claims they had to pay out? One of the reasons we chose Palm City, Florida, was because they had the reputation of never having hurricanes come ashore. After we moved in, we had three hurricanes in thirteen months: Francis, Jean, and Wilma.

One of the few times we were in Florida during the hurricane season was 2004. Earlier that year we had made the decision to sell our boat and upgrade to a more seaworthy vessel suitable for the Atlantic Ocean. We had dreams of taking our own boat to the Bahamas as well as the Florida Keys, and the Carver just was not suitable. We had made one trip to the Keys through the Okeechobee Waterway, which is a canal that connects the east coast of Florida to the west coast. We were about ninety miles of open water from Fort Myers to Key West, which was enough to tell us it was time to upgrade if we were going to cruise the Atlantic Ocean.

The hurricane warnings began with a storm, Wilma, forecast to hit the Florida coast, but it was not forecast to hit anywhere near our home. I was due to be in San Diego with my partner Chris to give a presentation to senior members of an Indian tribe. This was a big deal, with several hundred million dollars potentially at stake. I could not miss this meeting.

It was an overcast morning when Carol drove me to the Fort Lauderdale airport. We had an eerie feeling as we drove down I-95, where there was hardly any traffic. Even the tolls were suspended. The plan was for Carol to return after the trip to the airport and supervise the handyman installing the hurricane shutters. It was fortunate that we had already sold the boat and had not purchased a new one, so we did not have to make preparations for the boat as well as a house. Since we were not expecting a direct hit, we were putting up the shutters out of an abundance of caution. We also had a small Honda gasoline-powered generator that I used on the boat. It would produce enough electricity for about two lamps and the refrigerator. The handyman believed our preparation was overkill, but Carol persisted and eventually prevailed in getting him to put up the shutters for about half the house.

When Chris and I landed in San Diego, we went directly to the Indian reservation and checked into the casino hotel. We were given VIP treatment and comped the presidential suite. The suite consisted of two bedrooms and a large living/entertainment area. I took one of the rooms and was anxious to check the Weather Channel to determine the status of Hurricane Wilma—except there was no TV in my room. There were, however, several remote controls. I played around with each of them until miraculously I heard a noise coming from the foot of the bed, and a TV began to appear. I can remember thinking, wow, our clients must think we're more important than we are and maybe I should brush up on all the technology around us. To this day I'm technologically challenged and frustrated daily.

Once I had the Weather Channel tuned in, I discovered that the storm had taken an unexpected turn and was headed directly to the Treasure Coast of Florida, which was exactly where we lived. I immediately called Carol to find that she and Cheyenne were holed up in one of the closets with blankets on the floor, a battery/crank-operated radio that we had purchased for just this purpose, and a flashlight. In the middle of our discussion, while Carol was updating me, we lost cell service, and that was the last phone contact we had for two days.

GUT PUNCH

Unless you have been through a hurricane, there is nothing you can compare it to. I remember thinking how difficult it was to sit in Colorado and watch the hurricanes hit Florida. This time the two things I loved the most in life were barricaded in a closet, and I was two thousand miles away. This would never happen again. Whatever life would throw at us we would face together.

To add insult to injury, we did not get any business from the Indian reservation. It was a sad experience but an insight-producing one, nonetheless. The people that were handling the account were not producing competitive results. We did have our suspicions that someone was getting kickbacks at the time. One of the more startling facts we discovered was that at the time a child with Indian blood turns eighteen, he automatically received $6,000 monthly. This results in huge drug and alcohol problems. On woman relayed a story of how a young teenager she knew had a brand-new BMW. Apparently, he didn't like it after he drove it for a while. It ran out of gas while he was driving it, and he simply left it on the side of the road and went out and bought a new car—another example of how providing something for nothing is not helping people but actually hurting their efforts.

By the time Carol and I were able to make phone contact again, she had learned that the Fort Lauderdale airport was closed, but Orlando was open. She changed my flight immediately or it might have been days before I could have returned home.

Three days after the storm hit the Treasure Coast of Florida, she and Cheyenne picked me up in Orlando, and we returned to our home in Palm City, Florida. As we got closer to home, the surrounding area began to look more and more like a war zone, with fallen trees and power lines cluttering the landscape. We were able to get home. Our little generator was still powering our refrigerator and a few lamps in the house. We lived like that for a couple of days until power was restored and the clean-up began. Once again damage was minimal. We lost the screened pool enclosure and a few tiles from our roof. However, we were even more thankful we had been able to sell our boat before the storm hit because it totally destroyed our marina. It would be almost two years before it was restored.

CHAPTER 26

REFLECTIONS ON MOVING FOR THE TENTH TIME

By 2009 we had sold our Colorado home and moved into our Florida home. It was a bittersweet experience, and to this day, Carol and I reminisce about all the wonderful memories from our time in Colorado. I'm reminded of the old saying, "I'd rather be lucky than smart," as it applies once again. We were able to sell our Colorado house at the top of the market, shortly before the financial/housing crash hit. Within a short period of time, the Florida real estate market crashed, and two builders in our area closed shop.

344 SW Harbor View Drive, Palm City, Florida

For several years Carol and I had coveted the lot on the end of our street. A builder had begun building a spec house there when the financial crisis hit. He had three exterior concrete walls erected when the bank foreclosed. We were familiar with the floor plan because it had been used as a model for another high-end development in our area. We ultimately joined forces with a builder, bought it from the bank, modified the plans, and completed the house to our specifications.

In some ways the move was one of the easiest. The house we were moving from was located three doors down, and much of the move was completed by golf cart.

As mentioned earlier, we sold our Carver cruiser right before Hurricane Wilma hit Florida in 2004 and were boatless for the next few years. Once we were settled into one house, we were ready to get back into boating. After doing a little homework, we decided that Grady-White had a good reputation as an offshore cruising/fishing boat and ultimately bought a 330 Express and named it *Sir Reel*.

As a result of the purchase, we were made aware of the Grady-White owners' club in Vero Beach, the Grady Bunch. It was organized by the dealer in Vero Beach and composed of owners who were customers of Vero Marine, the dealer. The mission of the club was to provide an opportunity for new and old owners alike to share the experience of Grady-White ownership as well as the camaraderie and confidence building of cruising the Atlantic and the Caribbean and piloting your own vessels.

Members of the club possessed various levels of experience, running the gamut from novice to experienced boaters, but the old saying about there being safety in numbers applied to all when exposed to the elements of nature and the inevitable unforeseen hazards. It's comforting to know that there are others with you to provide the security blanket needed for the novice boater to gain experience. We ultimately joined the Grady Bunch as well as the Moorings Yacht Club in Vero Beach. The yacht club was a member of the Florida Council of Yacht Clubs, which was made up of over thirty clubs spread out along the coast of Florida, going from the panhandle down to around the tip of Florida and the Keys and north to almost the Florida-Georgia line. Membership in one provided reciprocity for all.

GUT PUNCH

While the Moorings Yacht Club was about an hour's drive by car and two hours by boat, it was the closest club to us. It was a great boating destination for weekend trips and holiday outings. Our membership in the Grady Bunch as well as the Moorings Yacht Club was the basis for friendships made that will last a lifetime. We had the opportunity to expand our cruising experience by making several trips to the Bahamas and the Florida Keys with the group, and eventually, as our confidence grew, we evolved into a smaller group of four or five boaters.

I remember one of my first impressions of the Grady Bunch. After returning home, Carol and I commented on the fact that all the people were so down to earth, and no one seemed to be too full of themselves. There were many trips before we would learn the more personal sides of the various members. Were they retired? If so, what did they do in life before they were retired? Some were still working. We would learn later that our group was made up of doctors and professionals involved in the citrus industry, the financial industry, marketing, and art, as well as a former presidential pilot and even a former Miller beer distributor.

It was on one of our first trips to the Bahamas that I learned even former presidential pilots like to have fun. All our boats were at anchor at a beach in the Abacos. My newly formed friendship with the pilot, Dennis, found us floating with the Mad Hatter. The Mad Hatter was an inflatable cooler that held some ice, drinks, and, of course, beer. Dennis and I floated leisurely in the crystal-clear water of the Caribbean, discussing everything from world affairs to pheasant hunting in South Dakota. With our backs to Dennis's anchored boat, we were totally unaware of the receding tide until it was too late.

Dennis ultimately became a client of Grant Koehler & Levin, and that experience has resulted in one of the closest and rewarding friendships in my life. Fifteen-plus years of annual pheasant-hunting trips in South Dakota and South Florida cruising have etched memories in my mind that will never be forgotten. A true and lifelong friendship—and he remained a client as well.

Later, when Carol and I were celebrating our twenty-fifth anniversary, Dennis presented us with the following.

HAPPY 25TH ANNIVERSARY

Life has a way of slipping by faster than we realize. Events such as birthdays, anniversaries and other memorable events set life's course with both family and friends.

Patty and I are honored you included us in celebrating your 25th.

GUT PUNCH

Friends are one of the most valuable commodities in this world. Friendship for us is magnetic. That is to say, when we met Carol and you in the living room of Bruce McIntyre's house in the 2005 Captains meeting for our first trip to the Bahamas, we immediately felt that magnetism of a friendship about to blossom. Well, that attraction has only allowed the roots of the blossom to grow deeply into the ground over the last 17 years. For us our friendship has grown from a blossom into a mighty oak tree. I believe it is rare today to have a friendship as the one we have nurtured together over the years.

I simply define friendship in the following way. If you called me at 3 a.m. and said, I need your help as soon as possible. I would hang up the phone, get in my car, drive to your house at break-neck speed, knock on your door and then and only then, would I ask why? I believe with all my heart that should the table be reversed, you too would do the same. We will enjoy your 25th tonight and have a gift for you both to enjoy it in the days, months and years to come. I desperately sought to find the perfect 25-year-old bottle of scotch and a truly special bottle of Chardonnay for you two to share and for you, Tom to enjoy the scotch on occasions you deem appropriate. I was not successful in finding that special 25-year-old bottle, but I did find a 32-year-old bottle of Dewar's.

To celebrate your 25th, the special Chardonnay and the 32-year-old Dewar's are our gift to both of you to be enjoyed for as long as the last. I now believe not finding a 25-year-old bottle of Scotch was and omen for good fortune in the years beyond you 25th. If you are prudent and reserve some of the scotch for celebrating years 26 through 32 with an ounce or so, it too will last until your 32nd Anniversary. However, I think that should it warm you pallet like I think it will, it may well not make it to your 26th Anniversary.

Enjoy and share both my true friends and again, thank you for including us in you celebration.

Dennis and Patti

Grady Bunch in Useppa Is

GUT PUNCH

Sir Reel II 36 Grady Express

Sir Reel III 44 Tiera Sport Fish

Over the next several years, we would upgrade our boat from the Grady-White 330 to a Grady-White 360 (*Sir Reel II*) and eventually to a Tiara 44 sportfish (*Sir Reel III*).

Up until 2020 our playground was the waters surrounding south Florida. We cruised the Florida coast, the Gulf of Mexico, and the Bahamas. We made regular trips to the West End, Bimini, Nassau, and the Abacos.

Hope Town, Bahamas, with *Sir Reel*, 33 Grady White Express

Hope Town, Green Turtle, Marsh Harbor, and Great Guana Cay, the home of Nippers, were among our favorites spots. Sadly, many of our favorite spots were wiped out as a result of Hurricane Irma hitting many parts of the Bahamas during the hurricane season of 2017. The destruction was so great that much of the islands has still not been rebuilt as I write this in 2021.

GUT PUNCH

While cruising the Bahamas became less desirable after Hurricane Irma left destruction in its path, South Florida, the Keys, and the west coast of Florida provided numerous fabulous destinations and great fishing experiences. The most enjoyable destinations were the Ocean Reef Club in Key Largo, where we were members for over ten years; a one-day trip on the Atlantic when weather permitted; or a two-day trip on the Intracoastal Waterway.

MY TWO BEST FISHING BUDDIES WITH OUR PRIZE CATCH

At one time we had so much fresh swordfish in our freezer that Carol grew so tired of it that to this day she can no longer eat swordfish.

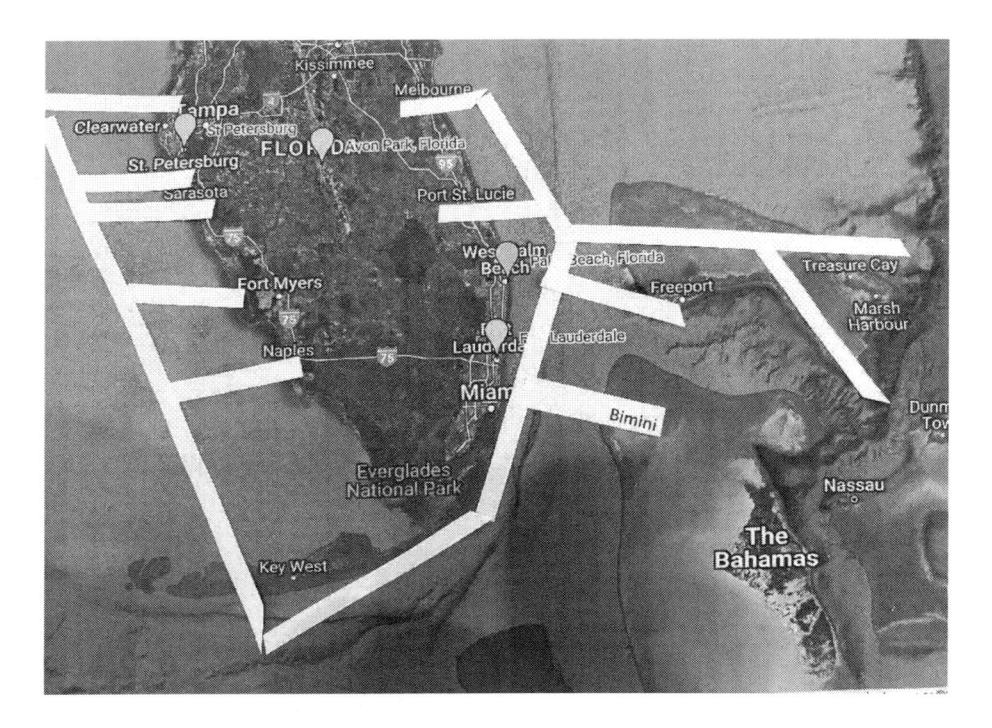

OUR CRUISING GROUNDS, 2007-2021

After almost forty years of boating, the balance scale between work and pleasure began to tilt, and the work involved began to take its toll. What I once viewed as enjoyable was slowly reaching the level of work. You can only see the crystal-clear blue water of the Caribbean so many times before it loses its luster. You can only eat so much Bahamian conch and drink so much rum. While the jury may still be out on the rum part of that observation, with age, the work/reward seemed to be skewing toward the work part of the equation.

While I was never a big fan of cruise ships, much preferring the freedom associated with piloting my own boat, it was at about this time that Carol signed us up for a Royal Caribbean cruise to the Eastern Caribbean. That cruise was followed by several more. While the rum tasted the same, the work/pleasure equation by far favored the pleasure side of the balance scale. That year we put only ten hours on our own boat, and I decided it was time to sell. With the exception of the brief time after Hurricane Wilma, this was the first time since the early 1980s I was boatless.

AND YES, THE RUM DID TASTE THE SAME AT FOXY'S IN JOST VAN DYKE.

CHAPTER 27

REFLECTIONS—WHAT HAPPENED TO THE AMERICA I GREW UP IN?

The last year and a half has been difficult. Daily activities changed the day I made the decision to sell the boat, resulting in an immediate increase in free time. Then with the diagnosis we began juggling calendars to keep up with all the doctor's appointments and immune therapy treatments. Free time took on a different role and meaning. It was just time to occupy the time I wasn't thinking about cancer and death, which often seemed to be all my time.

Fortunately, I was able to stay somewhat busy and active in our business by making day trades and doing some client consultations. Trying to stay current with the financial markets forced me to have the TV on most of the day. My motivation was to search out anything that could give me an advantage for future investments. The result was an overdose of news and politics. Although I was able to resist the addiction to some of the drugs used in my treatments and surgery, the timing couldn't have been worse. While I'm sure there is never a good time to be diagnosed with cancer, I'm sorry to say I became addicted, a political junkie.

My diagnosis was before the 2020 election. Consequently, I have been subjected to watching every painful day of the of the Biden administration, and I fear I am seeing the beginning of the end. After the first fourteen months of the Biden administration, I feel like I'm growing old in a country I no longer recognize. My dream is turning into a nightmare. As I write this, I am seventy-five, still part of the baby boom generation. Like my father, I believed in the American dream. We worked hard and paid our taxes. Today I feel like a stranger in a land that gets stranger by the day.

Our parents and our generation struggled to raise families. Some went to war, like our fathers and grandfathers before us, fighting for the concept of freedom and not wanting to be under the thumb of an oppressive government and not wanting to live off the government either. We were hoping to make things better for our children and grandchildren. Our parents could retire at sixty-five in the mortgage-free home they bought in their thirties. We're still working at seventy-five. Retirement is a distant dream. We're working to provide benefits for illegal immigrants, addicts, and loons who camp and defecate on the streets. Yet our leaders are unashamed of how we treat our veterans. Many are also living on the street after they gave up everything to fight for this country. Others are committing suicide at an alarming rate. In 2021 research found that 30,177 active-duty personnel and veterans who served in the military after 9/11 have died by suicide—compared to the 7,057 service members killed in combat in those same twenty years. That is, military suicide rates are four times higher than deaths that occurred during military operations.

A day doesn't pass that I am not contacted by some private organization for donations that should be the responsibility of the government and the tax dollars we give them. Seven million illegal immigrants coming over Biden's border will need jobs, health care, and education by the end of his first term. Our tax dollars that could be spent on our veterans are being spent on the Green New Deal.

Speaking of education, we have a Department of Education that is run by the teachers' union, an organization that believes it's more important to teach critical race theory than basic math, reading, science, and good old-fashioned American history. America is ranked ninth in reading and thirty-first in math.

Patriotism seems to be a thing of the past. I know many of my friends who are close to my age tear up and get a lump in their throat during the singing of the national anthem, yet the younger generation seems to be unaffected. Why? Parents of my generation were proud to be American. We started every school day with the Pledge of Allegiance. We all had friends or relatives who were killed in action defending this country. Now it seems we occupy our time tearing down America and dividing its citizens by race, sex, religion, and anything else that may help some politicians get votes. I truly doubt that if the time came, the current generation of millennials would be capable of defending anything. They are simply too concerned with being verbally offended God forbid a bullet strike them.

Most in my generation do not recognize Biden's America either. I'm not suggesting it's all his fault, because it has been happening for a long time. I think things started to change for the worse under Johnson and the "Great Society" and his war on poverty. That was when getting something for nothing, rather than working for it, began to take root. I compare this trend to a great avalanche. Back in the early 1960s, there were just a few rocks coming down the mountainside, but under Obama and now Biden, the whole mountain began to let loose. The "Great Society" was supposed to reduce and eliminate poverty. In 1965 the poverty rate in this country stood at 14 percent. Now, after untold trillions of dollars have been spent, the poverty rate is at 14.3 percent. The national debt in 1965 was $317 billion, with a debt-to-GDP ratio of 43 percent. Our national debt for the year ending 2021 was $29.6 trillion, with a debt-to-GDP ratio of 123 percent.

Our government is broken, and sometimes I feel like I'm the only one who cares. If you wonder about corruption in government, you need look no further than the Hunter Biden laptop scandal. You may want to broaden your investigation to include the Pelosi family as well. Investigation? Are you kidding? They don't investigate their own. The corruption is not limited to the Democrats either. How about Mitch McConnell's wife's connection to China?

There is no question in my mind that Obama squandered the greatest opportunity of his presidency. He was elected the first black president and was reelected to a second term. Don't talk to me about systemic racism. But instead of using the opportunity to unite us, he chose to divide, as evidenced by his famous beer summit where he chose to persecute the

Cambridge campus police for doing their job. That divisive rhetoric continued throughout his presidency.

Our military is led by men who are social workers and politically correct bureaucrats. They can't fight, but they're great at getting soldiers to use preferred pronouns and combating imaginary racism in the ranks. They allowed Biden to totally bungle the withdrawal from Afghanistan and are afraid to upset Putin in Ukraine. They say that race is a systemic problem in America. I repeat, we elected a black president in 2008, and he served for two terms. If we're white, we're told that we are responsible for every problem that plagues people of color. We're to blame for the roughly 70 percent of black children born out of wedlock. Apparently, we forced their parents to behave irresponsibly, just as cops are to blame for the deaths of thugs who threaten their lives. If you're pulled over, don't run or resist arrest. But if you do, it's my fault. Go figure? Savages and thugs who burn down cities are hailed as heroes and celebrated as warriors for social justice while the Department of Justice goes after parents in school board meetings speaking up for their kids. The mayors take down statues of Washington and Columbus and commission murals of George Floyd. If you're white you are also responsible for slavery, segregation, the Wounded Knee Massacre, and Japanese Americans interned during World War II. Racism is in our blood. Remember, throughout the course of human history, racism has never existed anywhere but here. Right?

While at Miller Brewing Company, I had many minorities working for me. One in particular worked very closely with me for my last ten years. We became very good friends, and in fact, as staffing changes were being made at the end, I tried to protect his position for as long as I could and extend his employment. If he was going to be let go, I wanted to be sure he got all the severance he was entitled to because his departure was out of his control. After we both left the company, we continued to hang out together and socialize together. He was with me the night I met Carol. Yet he recently called me a racist because my point of view was different from his on a topic. Maybe he is the racist.

Forget racial minorities. Now, we're told that there are "sexual minorities." We're told that a man who thinks he's a woman in fact is a woman and is entitled to use the lady's room with our daughters and granddaughters. We simply must accept it or be called homophobes.

And what passes for entertainment is sickening. All blood and gore and sadistic killers, and we wonder why our society is getting more dangerous. Some liberal loon came up with the idea to defund the police, and now they wonder why crime in our largest cities is out of control. As they say, you can't make this stuff up.

We search in vain for contemporary movies with characters we can admire. The void has given rise to Turner Classic Movies, with reruns from the forties and fifties. If you watched the 2022 Super Bowl halftime show, you saw our culture at its worst. I don't dance much anymore, but to be cool and current, I would have to spend half the time grabbing my crotch.

I believe that the cultural decay began with removing prayer from the schools in the early 1960s and a country that allowed partial-birth abortion.

In her book, *Serenity in the Storm*, Kayleigh McEnany does an excellent job describing the practice, politics, and court cases surrounding partial-birth abortion.

By the year 2000, President Bill Clinton had twice vetoed bills passed by the Republican congress that would have banned this heinous procedure. Twenty years ago there were two cases that received significant exposure. One was the case of Kermit Gosnell, commonly referred to as the abortion doctor, and the second was the Supreme Court case of *Stenberg v Carhart*, in which the Court struck down a Nebraska law banning the practice. The following descriptions may be graphic and difficult, but I found them so moving in McEnany's book that I decided to include them here to emphasize that there must be something terribly wrong with a society and its people for it to allow the practice to have continued for as long as it has. More concerning is that even today there are those who truly believe that the practice should not have been discontinued.

I'm going to restate some of the testimony in the two cases, asking the reader to keep in mind that, as similar and as graphic the testimony appears in both cases, in one case the doctor involved was convicted of murder and, in the second case, the Supreme Court found the Nebraska law outlawing the practice described unconstitutional. "The Gosnell case is about a doctor who killed babies and endangered women. What we mean is that he regularly and illegally delivered live, viable babies in the third trimester of pregnancy and then murdered these newborns by severing spinal cords with scissors."[2]

In her book, McEnany reports that Justice Kennedy, writing for the minority, correctly notes that "the fetus, in many cases, dies just as a human adult or child would: It bleeds to death as it is torn limb to limb. The fetus can be alive at the beginning of the dismemberment process and can survive for a time while its limbs are being torn off. This is a proposition that the abortion doctor, Dr. Carhart acknowledges. Dr. Carhart even went so far as to note that at times with extensive parts of the fetus removed, he has observed fetal heartbeat via ultrasound. Perhaps most troubling of all was Dr. Carhart's admission that he knows of a physician who removed the arm of the fetus only to have the fetus go on to be born as a living child with one arm."[3]

Think about what you just read. The Supreme Court of the United States heard a testimony from an abortion doctor that a heartbeat was evident as a baby was being torn apart limb by limb. They also heard about a baby born as a living child with one arm because his or her arms had been torn off during the D&E procedure. In spite of and totally unfazed by this, the Supreme Court voted 5–4 in *Stenberg v. Carhart* to strike down the Nebraska law banning the procedure. As you might imagine, the five in the majority were the liberal Democrat members of the court.

Thankfully, by the summer of 2022, the Supreme Court voted in a 6–3 majority to push the issue back to the states to decide. Unfortunately, some states would allow this heinous procedure to continue. It is unfathomable to me how someone who understands the procedure could support such legislation. I am proud that our state and governor were able to pass a fifteen-week, six-day limit.

Since the abortion issue seems to have moved front and center in our politics, I can't believe Democrats continue to advocate such evil. McEnany does an outstanding job describing the heinous procedure involved in late

---

[2] Conor Friedersdorf, "Why Dr. Kermit Gosnell's trial should be a Front-Page Story." *The Atlantic*, April 12, 2013, https://tinyurl.com/mr3d4e8c.

[3] *Kayleigh McEnany, Serenity in the Storm* (: Liberatio Protocol, 2023), 101-102.

term abortion in her book *Serenity in the Storm*, specifically between pages 97 and 111. In my opinion if you want to understand the moral decay of our country you need only look to the policies presented by the Socialist Democratic Party of America.

On top of living in a country that's unrecognizable, we can't even afford to live here anymore. That can be traced directly to the Biden administration. You need a second mortgage to buy a steak. A hamburger and fries at McDonald's is a gourmet feast. Filling up the tank is agonizing. Paying confiscatory taxes marks us as serfs. The week before Biden took office, we were energy independent and shipping energy to other countries. On the day he took office, with the stroke of a pen he reversed the Trump energy policies, and the price of oil began to rise.

Biden wants to blame energy and inflation costs on Putin's war in Ukraine. How dumb does he think we are? Putin continues to ship 670,000 barrels of oil a day while Biden lets our pipelines rust and our oil, coal, and natural gas remain the ground. Then he goes hat in hand to the Saudis and Venezuelans to beg for more imports and asks Russia to assist in the negotiations with Iran. As they say, you can't make this stuff up. Oh, I said that already. The cost to the American consumer is justified by the government's new infatuation with the Green New Deal and electric cars for everyone.

Earlier I said that our government is broken, and while I blame the socialist liberal Democrats for much of our broken country, the Republicans are not blameless either. There is enough incompetence to go around but based on the Biden administration's performance in its first year, the Democrats are proving conclusively that they are leading the pack when it comes to idiots in the party. Both sides put party before country, and therein lies the problem. Instead of concentrating on the real problems the country faces, they worry about their own power and getting reelected.

Going into the 2022 and 2024 elections, in my opinion, the four biggest problems the nation faces are cultural decay, illegal immigration, inflation/energy, and China. Everyone supports legal immigration. I would not be here if it were not for legal immigration. My great-great-grandparents emigrated from Germany. My great-great-grandfather came by ship first and waited two years for my great-great-grandmother to join him in New York, where they finally reconnected and walked across the United States to settle a farm in the Midwest. They buried their first child in a field in Ohio. President Trump had the border problem and energy under control. If Biden goes unchecked, 15 percent of the American population will be illegal immigrants by the end of his first term. To fix the problem, all Biden would have to do is swallow his pride and return to the Trump policies that worked. Instead, he puts the whole country at risk to broaden the Democratic base of his party, and Congress does nothing. Treasonous!

China, however, is a little more complicated. My fear is that most of the politicians are too busy trying to keep their power and get reelected. They waste their time on critical race theory and passing legislation that would allow men to use the women's restrooms and are totally unaware of the vast problem we face with China. Because of President Trump's business acumen, he was beginning to get a handle on the issues. But bumbling Biden and his administration are clueless.

From those who have traveled to China, I am told that it is clean and safe, and there is no welfare. No universal medical care. In the eighth grade, all students take an exam. The top 40 percent go to high school, and the bottom 60 percent go to trade schools.

China's weapon of choice to conquer the world is finance, and countries around the world are falling fast. In the near future, China will employ millions of American workers and dominate thousands of small communities all over the United States. Chinese acquisitions of US companies continue at a rapid pace. The Smithfield Foods acquisition is a great example. Smithfield Foods is the largest pork producer and processor in the world. It has facilities in twenty-six US states, and it employs tens of thousands of Americans. It directly owns 460 farms and has contracts with about 2,100 others. A Chinese company bought it for $4.7 billion, and that means that the Chinese are now the most important employer in dozens of rural communities all over America.

It is important to keep in mind that there is not much of a difference between "the Chinese government" and "Chinese corporations." In 2011, 43 percent of all profits in China were produced by companies where the Chinese government had a controlling interest. Recently a Chinese company spent $2.6 billion to purchase AMC Entertainment, one of the largest movie theater chains in the United States. Chinese companies control more movie ticket sales than any other entity in the world.

China is not just relying on acquisitions to expand its economic power. For example, Golden Dragon Precise Copper Tube Group recently broke ground on a $100 million plant in Thomasville, Alabama. Many of the residents of Thomasville will be glad to have jobs, but it will also become yet another community heavily dependent on communist China. In addition, China is setting its sights on Detroit and the auto industry, producing everything from seat belts to shock absorbers. It is also interested in acquiring energy resources in the United States. For example, China is actually mining for coal in the mountains of Tennessee. Guizhou Guochuang Energy Holding Group spent $616 million to acquire Triple H Coal Company in Jacksboro, Tennessee.

Are you starting to get the picture? China is on the rise and has been for a long time, while America plays political games. Over the past decade, the United States has run a trade deficit with China that comes to almost 4 hundred billion annually. China currently holds almost $1 trillion of the $28.9 trillion US national debt. China has more foreign currency reserves than any other country. China now produces more than twice as many automobiles as does the United States. China now consumes more energy than does the United States. China is now, in aggregate, the leading manufacturer of goods in the entire world. China is now the number one producer of wind and solar in the world. China produces three times as much coal and eleven times as much steel as the United States does. China produces more than 90 percent of the global supply of rare earth elements. And most importantly, China is now the number one supplier of components that are critical to the operation of any national defense system.

This, to me, is the epitome of the incompetence of the 535 members of Congress and an out-of-touch president. Not only do the Chinese have an excess amount of influence in our national defense, but they also have an undue amount of influence in the pharmaceutical industry. What's in your medicine? Inside every pill are active and inactive ingredients. The active ingredients create the therapeutic effect. In regular-strength Tylenol, the active ingredient is acetaminophen. Without it the pills would be ineffective. China is the largest global supplier of the chemical building blocks needed to make many prescriptions drugs, over-the-counter products, and vitamins. If you take a vitamin C pill with your morning coffee, it probably contains Chinese components. Virtually all penicillin has Chinese components.

It's time our politicians start putting America first, before their respective political parties. You would think they could at least agree on these important issues. I fear our political system is broken. If things don't change, I think I may start learning Chinese as a second language. It is becoming more and more obvious to me as I am exposed to the idiocy of Joe Biden and his administration day after day that the danger to America is not Joe Biden but a citizenry capable of entrusting a man like him with the presidency. In the last election, it came down to a very capable person with policies that were working but who tweeted too much and an incompetent politician who has spent his whole life living off the taxpayer, campaigned from his basement, and never accomplished anything on his own.

The republic can survive Biden, who is, after all, merely a fool. Kamala Harris is totally incompetent. It is less likely to survive a multitude of fools, such as those who made him their president. I cannot understand why the liberal progressive Democrats continue to strive so vigorously to make America a socialist state.

Our senator from Florida recently said, "I don't understand why a system of ideology that has failed everywhere in the world that it's been tried has only brought misery and suffering and exiled refugees. Why would you ever want any element of that to be a part of our politics here. It's always existed. There's always been people out there that believe in these things and want to ruin this country." We look in vain for the courageous leaders of the past. People like Ronald Reagan; A Lincoln or Teddy Roosevelt or JFK. If JFK were alive today, he would be a Republican. Our leaders of the past would at least put country over party.

Trump came with many faults, but no one could ever question whether he was putting America first. More importantly, he had financial strength to take on both parties and break up the good old boys' club known as Congress. He recognized what was wrong inside our government and was willing to take it on. It is unlikely that the multitude of fools who voted against his tweets will somehow see the ignorance of their position.

While I have always tried to stay current with the political scene, the impact of my relentless exposure to twenty-four-hour news has heightened my awareness of the sad state of affairs our country is in. It has provided me with a potential avenue of interest and potential volunteer opportunities, if and when cancer ceases to be my major concern.

There has been a second benefit to all the exposure to the talking heads. Someone I started to follow because of his no-bullshit attitude and "tell it like it is" ethos was Dan Bongino, a Fox News Contributor. I learned he was also a resident of our community, and we actually go to the same church. He was diagnosed with cancer about the same time I was. I met him in person one time while we were waiting in line at a restaurant, and I found him to be very friendly and pleasant. He is a former New York City policeman and worked in the Secret Service protecting Obama. One night he had an author on by the name of Lee Strobel who wrote *The Case for Christ*. Bongino promoted it as a book that made the biggest impact in his life. With a recommendation like that, I thought I would give it a try.

CHAPTER 28

REFLECTIONS ON FAITH

When you are diagnosed with cancer, it's very hard not to think about death. When I think about death, I think about God and religion. When I was a child, God and religion played an important part in my family's lives. Sunday school, church, catechism on every Saturday morning during the school year during my freshman and sophomore years in high school. My family went to church every Sunday. When I went away to college, things changed, but I still went periodically.

When Carol and I got married, I again began going to church with Carol. Carol has a strong faith. Even when we were dating, we went to church together. Since we married, we have been going to mass just about every Sunday. I mention this so I do not give you the impression that because of cancer I found religion; I had strong religious beliefs before my diagnosis.

Thinking back, I believe my faith was more of a blind faith developed and influenced by the various inputs I have had since childhood. With the onset of the cancer diagnosis, I sure prayed daily to be cured. But I think I was learning I wanted something more. Before I knew it, I had downloaded Bongino's book recommendation and was deep into the author's investigation of Christ. Coincidentally, my reading would occur during the Lenten season. Do you believe in omens?

The author Lee Strobel was a lawyer and an investigative journalist. It soon became obvious that he had researched his topic extensively and supported most of his findings with facts, common sense, and logic. As a result, I took a moment to determine exactly what I expected to get from reading the book. Reinforcement of the blind-faith beliefs I already held. No. Or information that will help me move my blind faith to something more tangible, supported by facts and logical thinking, thereby limiting the blind-faith aspect of my thinking?

I soon learned that the author took painstaking care in supporting his conclusions with multiple sources, not just his own opinion. Normally I don't enjoy books that have more footnotes than dialogue; this seemed different. The footnotes and the added references made the observations more understandable and conclusions reasonable. The format the author chose was in keeping with his legal training, and it seemed like he was preparing for a court case.

Because of my religious indoctrination during my youth, I did have a basic understanding of Christianity. While I was brought up as a Lutheran, I have been going to the Catholic church for the last thirty years. My Lutheran religious experience was with the Missouri Synod, which, with some minor exceptions, I found to be very similar to Catholicism.

I found the *Case for Christ* to be exactly what I was looking for. It provided me with tangible facts that I could use to support the framework of my beliefs. First, any discussion of God and religion must begin with the study of the Bible. The holy book was written over a period of 1,600 years and contains sixty books by forty authors. These authors were from all walks of life. Two of them were half-brothers of Jesus, who did not believe his claims until after they witnessed the crucifixion and resurrection.

Despite the diversity of its authors and being written over a period of 1,600 years, and although most of the authors did not have access to the others' writing, the Bible displays a consistency of fact as well as theology. Not one of the authors criticized any of the others, and scholars have found that there were no dissenting opinions. In addition, *The Dead Sea Scrolls* were discovered in 1947, and these scrolls contained portions of all the books of Hebrew scriptures with the exception of the book of Esther. They contained the entire book of Isaiah. Scroll dates range from the third century BCE (before Christ) to the first century. About 230 manuscripts are referred to as biblical scrolls. These are copies of works that are part of the Hebrew Bible (The Leon Levy Dead Sea Scrolls Digital Library).

GUT PUNCH

Strobel interviewed thirteen scholars in preparation for his book. One, Lapides, identified more than four dozen major predictions in the Old Testament. Jesus of Bethlehem, born of a virgin, was pierced in the hands and feet upon crucifixion, even though that hadn't quite been invented yet as a standard punishment. Many scholars have tried to calculate the odds of the Old Testament prophecies being fulfilled in the person of Jesus Christ. Strobel writes that Peter Stoner, a writer and professor in Mathematics and astronomy, calculated that the chance of fulfilling just one of the Old Testament prophecies was one in ten to the seventeenth power.

Historians and scholars have determined that the Gospel of Mark was written no later than about AD 60, maybe even the late fifties. If Jesus was put to death in between thirty to thirty-three years of age, we're talking about a maximum gap of thirty years or so. Consider that, as I write this, JFK was killed in 1963, a full sixty years after the event. Few would consider accuracy to be a problem if someone were writing an account of the event today. Granted, today the writer would be aided by technology, but personal observation would still be available from firsthand accounts of something so significant. The assassination of a president, I think, would rank right up there with the crucifixion and resurrection of Christ.

Strobel tells us that the Gospels were written after almost all the letters of Paul, whose writing ministry probably began in the late forties. It's important to remember that Paul was not one of the original twelve apostles. He founded several Christian communities in the forties to the mid-fifties, and his conversion was estimated to be about AD 32. This would have occurred within two to five years of the crucifixion and resurrection. He makes a strong case that the Christian belief, though not written down, can be dated to within two years of the very event. These were the kinds of things that I was looking for to provide the underpinning of my faith. The author also addresses circumstantial evidence that, when presented in a court of law, may be meaningless, but I'm sure if I was on the jury such evidence would certainly have had an impact on my thinking. He points out that the historical records confirm the darkness at the time of the crucifixion. Scientist were unable to draw a correlation to an eclipse or any other atmospheric conditions. To further investigate the phenomenon of darkness, Strobel pursued the topic with one of his expert witnesses, Yamauchi, who quoted the scholar Paul Maier in his 1968 book *Pontius Pilate:* "This phenomenon evidently, was visible in Rome, Athens, and the other Mediterranean cites. It was a cosmic or world event. Phlegon, a Greek author from Caria writing of chronology soon after AD 137 reported that in the fourth year of the 2020nd Olympiad (i.e. AD 33). There was the greatest eclipse of the sun, and that it became night in the sixth hour of the day (i.e. noon) so that the stars even appeared in the heavens. There was a great earthquake in Bithynia, and many things were overturned in Nicaea."[4]

As I continued to read on and, in fact, study the contents of the book, I soon realized how little I actually knew. I'd considered myself a strong believer, yet I continued to learn things I would have thought a believer like me should already know. Did I learn these things as a child and simply forget? Was the influence of the Church and my parents so strong that it created the belief system that I have today without the underpinnings I now was searching for? Are those influences today being marginalized so that we are creating generations of young people without the moral groundings that existed in our past?

At seventy-five I thank God for the parents I had and the guidance they provided me. I fear that in many cases it is absent in parenting today. I didn't know that the apostle Paul never met Jesus prior to Jesus's death, but he said he did encounter the resurrected Christ and later consulted with some of the eyewitnesses to make sure he was spreading the same message they were. Because he began writing his New Testament letters years before the gospels were written down, they contain extremely early reports concerning Jesus. He was like an early-days Fox News reporter trying to be fair and balanced—so early that nobody can make a credible claim that his reports had been seriously distorted by legendary development. Some scholars believe that Paul's letters represent valuable external verification of the traditions about Jesus. I guess I should have known that he authored the two Timothy

---

4 Paul I. Maier , Pontius Pilat (lWheat, Ill.:Tyndale house , 1968b366, citing a fragment form Phelgon, Olympiads he Chronika 13, ed Otto KellerR3rum Naturalium Scriptures Graici Minores, 1(Leipsig: Teurber 1877)101.Translation by Maier.

books, Thessalonians, Colossians, Philippians, Ephesians, Galatians, two Corinthian books, and Romans. I do now.

I didn't intend to include a book report in my memoirs, but because I found this book to be so compelling in strengthening my already strong beliefs, I thought it appropriate. I can't imagine going through life without having God in it. For someone suffering from both the emotional and the physical stresses of cancer, for me, the stress is unimaginable. I hope these thoughts of faith might help others as it did me. For me, there is a peacefulness I find in my belief. I can call on it anytime.

From the day of my diagnosis, God has given me hope in so many ways. I believe that without God there is no hope. Many people struggle with the concept of God. For me, God is half the equation between love and hate. Do you believe in love? Of course, you do. Anyone that has observed the love between a mother and her child, a child and their parents, husbands and wives, or even humans and a pet know very well that love is alive and well in the world today. The other half of the equation is the devil, or evil and hate. We certainly would not question the existence of evil in the world when we see it all around us every day. By my logic, why would we then question the existence of God?

As soon as we began to communicate to friends and family that I had cancer, my support system kicked in. As you might have expected, first to the fight was Carol, one of the most positive people I know and the most important person in my life. There is no place for negativity in her being. "Don't worry, Pookie"—her nickname for me—"we're going to beat this thing," she said. A dear friend sent me a mass card with a novena that she and her husband had found in church when he was diagnosed with cancer. She said she and her husband prayed the prayer on the card every day. I started doing the same thing the day I received it. It must have worked for him, because he has been living a very fulfilled and happy life for as long as I have known him. Not surprisingly, my mother-in-law, who goes to mass every day, just smiled and said, "You're going to be just fine." Well-wishes and prayers started coming in from all over the country, providing positive encouragement.

Hope is a promise for the future. Maintaining a positive attitude is very important when fighting cancer. Mentally accepting the outcome is just as important, and when you have a strong faith in God, that acceptance is a given. Much like Jesus had to accept the Crucifixion, his death, and his resurrection, so do we have to accept the choices God has made for us. He has given us rational minds to make the right decisions in our lives. But we must remember that some of those decisions are out of our hands and up to God.

As word of my cancer spread throughout our network of friends, we began to hear numerous stories of the multiple cases where her friends were now cancer-free or successfully in remission. Those real-life examples are the hope or promise for the future that adds credibility to the process. The medical technology today is truly astounding.

Coincidentally, my good friend Dennis told me of a new drug he had just learned of through a friend. He told me the results of the tests to date and was curious about my opinion on it as a potential investment. He set up a call with the group that was behind the offering. The more we learned about the potential drug, the more interested we became. The CEO contacted me and explained to me where they were in their start-up and pending plans, from both a scientific and a financial point of view. He told me their lead product had completed all the preclinical work needed to file an investigational new drug application with the FDA and expected to be in clinical trials and Moffitt soon. He indicated that they were collaborating with Moffitt and Duke University.

There were too many coincidences for me to sit on the sidelines. My experience with Moffitt has been stellar. While I don't usually make investment decisions on coincidence, this time was an exception. Dennis and I spent considerable time on the phone, talking about investing in something that could truly make a difference in people's lives. He made the decision first. A few days later, I woke up in the morning, thinking, what if Dennis hits a home run on this investment? I'll be kicking myself for the rest of my life, however long that may be.. Not the best investment logic in the world, but what the hell. The investment consisted of a convertible note that would later be converted to preferred stock. Hopefully someday in the future the company will go public and we can cash in. We can only hope.

As part of my research, I learned that one of the areas in which the new drug was being studied was how it might increase the effectiveness of an immune therapy drug called Keytruda when it begins to lose its effectiveness. As indicated earlier, this is the same drug I am on for my immune therapy. Coincidence? Maybe. As I write this, the convertible note has now been converted to the preferred stock, and trials at Moffitt have begun. I remember thinking, How cool would it be that not only would Dennis's and my investment help save the lives of other people but might just save mine as well? My conversation with Dennis came at a time when I was feeling pretty low. The investment, however, helped me get back on track and see another glimmer of hope. Coincidence? Maybe.

My type of cancer was previously treated by chemotherapy, but over the years, chemo was found to be ineffective as a treatment. Sold under the brand name Keytruda, pembrolizumab is a humanized antibody used in cancer immunotherapy that treats melanoma, lung cancer, kidney cancer, and others. Like chemo, it is given by slow injection into a vein. Since I had both kidney cancer and melanoma, I was very fortunate to have one treatment that had an effective track record in treating both.

If you were to go online, as I did, and check the possible side effects of the drug, you would find an extensive list that includes tiredness; pain, including pain in muscles; rash; diarrhea; fever; cough; decreased appetite; itching; shortness of breath; constipation; pain in bones or joints and the stomach area; nausea; and low levels of thyroid hormone. Luckily for me, apart from minor nausea and stiffness in my neck, my side effects were minimal.

CHAPTER 29

REALITY—LIVING WITH CANCER: NOVEMBER 2021

It has now been approximately one year since I was diagnosed with cancer and this journey began. When I started to chronicle it, I had no idea where it would lead or if I would be around to finish my writing. From the night of the life-changing phone call until now, I still feel my life is on hold and I continue to live under a cloud. It's hard to describe, but the loss of purpose in one's life accompanies living with cancer. One seems preoccupied with the thought, How much time do I have left?

I have always been goal oriented (remember the powder blue GTO). That sense of lost purpose, in my case, was offset by the writing of these memories. It was cathartic in a way I didn't anticipate. Writing, in a way, allows you to relive your life again. That thought process forces you to focus on something other than cancer; it forces you to, once again, spend time thinking of all those memories that make up your life experiences. It gives you an opportunity to look back and say, Wow! Maybe you even appreciate it more than when you were actually living it. What a life I had! But it's not over. Now I must learn to live the life I have as a cancer patient and cherish each day that remains.

On November 30, 2021, I received my thirteenth immune therapy treatment and the results of my most recent CT scan. While the oncologist from the Moffitt team indicated that it was too early to tell, the CT scan was clear, and that was a good sign. She recommended that I continue my treatments for the duration of the year ending March 2022. We would need to do a PET scan in March and then reevaluate.

Cancer remission means that the signs and symptoms of cancer are reduced. Remission can be partial or complete. In a complete remission, all signs and symptoms of cancer have disappeared. If you remain in a complete remission for five years or more, some doctors may say you are cured.

So once again my life would be put on hold for the next four months. The month of March 2022 was busy. I had MRIs for my brain, chest, and abdomen and another CT scan for my kidney and lung area. Finally, the virtual visit with Moffitt and my Moffitt oncologist, Dr. Eroglu was finally scheduled for 3:00 p.m. on March 31, 2022.

It's hard to believe, but it has now been a year and a half since my diagnosis. My life seems like it has permanently been put on hold, and now once again, I wait for the Zoom call to begin. At 4:00 p.m. the nurse finally connects and tells me the doctor has been delayed and it will be another hour before she will be available. I guess the one thing I have learned on this journey is patience.

When she finally connects at 5:00 p.m., the waiting is over, and she tells me that the scans are clear and the Keytruda treatments can be discontinued. My cancer is officially in complete remission. She cautions me, however, that the cancer could reoccur at any time and I will need to do scans every three months for the foreseeable future.

I had been holding my breath while she spoke, awaiting her prognosis. I think when I finally exhaled, the neighbors down the street could hear me. While it was a tremendous relief to know that, at least for the short term, my cancer is in remission, it still is a burden to know that the cells are still inside my body and could resurface at any time.

While I'm thankful for the remission of the kidney cancer and melanoma, I am still faced with the remaining battle with prostate cancer. I had been mentally preparing myself to face whatever treatment would be required—only to receive another gut punch once again. That same week, as a result of a recent bimonthly check-up at my dermatologist, we discovered I have skin cancer on my lower eyelid. The cancer was in the form of a small growth about the size of a pinhead located adjacent to where the lash attaches to the lid. In addition to the spot on the eyelid, the dermatologist also found a spot on my leg that needed to be removed. Thankfully, the surgeries were successfully completed in August 2022 with no other complications.

Now only one obstacle remains, the prostate biopsy, which is scheduled for October 11, 2022. Keep the faith: progress is being made. I feel like I have been taking two steps forward and one step back for the last two years. But at least there is progress. I'm learning that there is life after a cancer diagnosis.

Fast forward to October 19, 2022. Once again, I learned I'm about to take several steps backward. The results of the prostate biopsy indicated the cancer is growing and needs to be addressed. And the beat goes on.

One of the most frequent comments throughout my cancer journey, regardless of whether it was regarding the kidney cancer, melanoma in my lung, or now prostate cancer, has been, "Tom, you're fortunate that you're dealing with cancer today and not several years ago. So much progress has been made." Hearing it so often caused me to do a little research. I was surprised to learn that according to the National Cancer Institute, back in 1775 Percivall Pott identified a relationship between exposure to chimney soot and one of the first incidences of squamous cell carcinoma of the scrotum among chimney sweeps. Mastectomy to treat breast cancer goes back to 1882, and Marie and Pierre Curie's discovery of radioactive elements radium and polonium was the gateway to radiation therapy, one of the successful cancer treatments used today. I learned that the hormonal therapy I would begin the second week of November 2022 goes back to a 1941 discovery by Charles Huggins, who found that removing the testicles to lower testosterone production or administering estrogens causes prostate tumors to regress. My doctor had informed me early on that testosterone was the lifeblood for prostate cancer.

Thankfully the procedure no longer involves the removal of testicles, but it does involve the lowering of testosterone through injection of estrogen and other hormonal applications. My treatment will involve several hormone shots, one before the beginning of the radiation treatments and then more later. The radiation treatment will be administered five days a week for a total of eight weeks. That's the bad news. The good news is that treatments are only fifteen to twenty minutes in duration.

Prostate cancer is the second leading cause of cancer death for men in the United States. There were basically two options of treatment for me. The doctor explained that they usually recommend surgery for men under seventy-five and radiation for men seventy-five and over. People treated with the external-beam radiation therapy have a cure rate of 95 percent for intermediate-risk prostate. During the 1970s about one in two people diagnosed with cancer survived at least five years. Now, more than two out of three survive that long. Today there are more than fourteen million cancer survivors in the United States alone.

While currently in remission, my melanoma is still an ongoing concern. This highly aggressive form of skin cancer is the fifth most common cancer in men and women in the United States. While more than 90 percent of melanomas are discovered early and removed by surgery, leading to positive results, this cancer may be lethal if it spreads to other parts of the body, like the liver, brain, or, in my case, lungs. Since the emergence of immunotherapy drugs called checkpoint inhibitors, the prognoses for those with metastatic melanoma have improved considerably. These drugs have improved survival and produced positive outcomes for many melanoma patients, most famously former president Jimmy Carter, who was diagnosed in 2015 with metastatic melanoma that had spread to his brain. Carter, now ninety-eight, was still able to keep a rigorous schedule and even continue building houses with no evidence of melanoma after doctors treated him with radiation therapy and the checkpoint inhibitor Keytruda. Sound familiar?

President Carter's good-news story has become very common since 2011, when the FDA approved the first checkpoint-inhibitor drug. Deaths from melanoma will continue to fall in the decades to come. It's interesting to note that melanoma deaths are dropping even as the number of new cases has risen sharply, as early detection methods have gotten better. The number of people who have had cancer has gone up greatly over the last fifty years in the United States. In 1971 there were three million people with cancer. According to the latest figures, as of 2022, there were eighteen million people living with a history of cancer in the United Sates. About 67 percent of cancer survivors have survived five or more years after diagnosis. About 18 percent have survived twenty or more years after diagnosis, and 64 percent of survivors are age sixty-five or older.

In addition to early detection, treatments are also improving. Treatments like surgery, radiation therapy, and chemotherapy are being used in better ways. Newer treatments such as targeted therapy and immunotherapy are extending and saving lives. Control of side effects has also improved greatly and can help keep planned treatments on schedule and help with patients' well-being.

The risk of death from cancer dropped by about 2 percent per year from 2015 to 2019 compared to about 1 percent a year during the 1990s. The number of cancer survivors is projected to increase by 24.4 percent to 22.3 million by 2032, compared to 18.1 million in 2022. The same research indicated between 2015 and 2019, overall death rates decreases by 2.1 percent per year for men and women combined.

I'm happy to report that by the time this book is published my radiation treatments were successful.

CHAPTER 30

REFLECTIONS ON PURPOSE VERSUS MOTIVATION

Ever since that powder blue GTO became part of my psyche, I thought I lived a life driven by purpose. I now believe that for most of my life, I have confused purpose with motivation. Early in my youth, the powder blue GTO motivated me to achieve. Status, career success, title, and financial comfort were not my purpose but my motivation. Later in life my position became my identity. I remember that after being terminated by Miller, for a while I lost my identity. "Senior vice president of sales" had been who I was. Now I was just Tom Koehler.

It took quite a while for me to realize that I was so much more than a title. While those things were all very important, they were simply various forms of measurement that society, unfortunately, has used to describe people and measure their implied worth. I always considered myself an achiever. Did this mean I was any less an achiever, a failure?

As I look back, my termination was merely a detour, an opportunity for more achievements to come. But at the time it was very difficult to accept. Only now, after the last three-year battle with cancer in various forms, do I look at my life and try to differentiate between purpose and motivation. In a way, purpose for now is quite simple: Be a good person. Be a good husband and friend, and be faithful to God.

With God's help and my motivation, I was able to achieve a lifestyle that hopefully would allow me to not be a burden to others and still allow us to live a comfortable, fulfilling, and rewarding life. It was this discovery because of a conversation that Carol and I had on the eve of my seventy-fifth birthday that helped me clarify the elusive purpose. In the end, it doesn't have to be so complicated, but rather simply something we do that makes us feel good about ourselves—not what we have but who we are. Would I rather be remembered as someone that was a good person and a good leader, who was compassionate and caring, or as someone that achieved some type of title in life and had a good bank account and adopted the arrogance that so often accompanies this so-called success?

Now that God has given me an opportunity to perhaps have a few more years, I hope to let my new discovery of purpose play a different role in my life. What I have really discovered, at least for me, is that for purpose to be meaningful, it must be combined with productivity. To be a good person and a productive one really is what causes me to feel good about myself. Because of the financial services business that we started over twenty years ago, I have never really retired. Because of two hardworking and dedicated partners, I have been able to stay active, which for me helps to fill the void between purpose and productivity. While productivity, for me, is a big part of my newly defined purpose, one element of purpose remained: helping others.

A very vivid example of that occurred for me while writing this book. Remember when I discussed the caregiver for Mr. Mike with, shall we say, less than scrupulous motivations—i.e., marriage and being included in Mr. Mike's will? When Mr. Mike and I first started discussing the possibility, before I became suspicious, he was planning on possibly opening an investment account for her and then adding to the accounts each year as warranted. Because of my concern regarding the motivation of one of the caregivers, I was reluctant and convinced Mr. Mike to delay the process. At that point the discussion was between him and me, with nothing in writing.

The caregiver who ultimately worked with Mr. Mike for the next five years was a blessing. Mr. Mike has since died, but I was still able to reward this caregiver for the compassion and loving care. To her he was like a father.

With nothing in writing, I approached Mr. Mike's heirs and related the story. They readily agreed, and we were able to carve out a sizable amount of Mr. Mike's estate for her. It was the right thing to do, and I compliment the heirs on their willingness and generosity.

As I write this, the estate has yet to be settled, so the caregiver has not received the gift Mr. Mike would have wanted her to have. I can't imagine the happiness and joy she will feel when she receives the news. I know that this would not have happened without my involvement, and the satisfaction I feel from helping her is one of the most rewarding feelings I have had in a long time. My new understanding of having purpose and being a good person provides all the motivation I need.

Helping others can manifest itself in many ways. Working with legitimate charities was where Carol and I began our efforts. Estate planning seems to go hand in hand with any cancer diagnosis. You naturally want to get your affairs in order. While I was going through the immune therapy, we also began to do just that. Because we have no children, in many ways it was harder. How far into the extended family do we bequeath? When my mom and dad died, I was left a small inheritance. At the time, by most people's measure, I was successful in my own right, and I decided that as a tribute to my mom and dad, I would start a family charitable foundation and use the money they gave me to help others: a fitting tribute to the two people who taught me so much. Over the years the funds were invested in the stock market and grew. The tax laws required that the foundation disperse a minimum of the proceeds each year. We had done this for the last twenty years.

When I was first diagnosed, we decided to close the foundation because of the extra work and responsibility for Carol if something should happen to me. We felt that dealing with the issues associated with my cancer would be challenging enough. The estate planning process changed all that, and we elected not to close the foundation but rather keep it open, with Carol continuing the giving process. The objective was to provide adequate funds for Carol's future financial security and long-term care if the need arose. Any funds remaining would be allocated to beneficiaries that would be determined through the ongoing research and planning that Carol and I would do beginning almost immediately.

We were so thankful and relieved that my cancer was in remission and for the role that Moffitt played in that process that first and foremost we decided we would provide funds to Moffitt to be used in their cancer research. Subsequently we have made significant contributions during some of their fundraising efforts using foundation funds that were still currently available. Developing a list of charities in addition to Moffitt is work in progress as I am writing this book, but to date our research includes a combination of major national charities like Tunnel to Towers and Saint Jude Children's Hospital and, naturally, our local church. While the funds available now are minimal, we hope that they will grow and when combine with our estate, someday they will be big enough to make a difference.

Our research revealed some unique local charities, like the Equine Rescue and Adoption Foundation (ERAF) and Big Dog Ranch, as well. ERAF, located in Palm City, Florida, has been in business for more than twenty years. It provides service to at-risk horses, but up until Carol and I started our research we were completely unaware of it. People actually abandon horses. Some are pets that people were no longer able to care for. Some are racehorses that are no longer able to race. As a previous horse owner (me) and animal lovers (both of us), we were amazed and immediately drawn to the organization. A visit to their website captured our interest. It read as follows:

> We are the beginning for horses who have been neglected, abused or surrendered by their owners and are in desperate need of help. Too often they come to us broken in spirit and without a safe home. Sometimes they come to us heart broken, grieving the loss of their human partner and longtime home. Very often they come to us ill or physically broken. The story is repeated time and again.
>
> With our hard work, your generosity, and a loving new home they can once again be healthy horses that are filled with life and promise. Our work is often filled with unspeakable sadness as the once upon a time majestic horses that have been abused, starved, and left unwanted come through our gates.

GUT PUNCH

Then comes that amazing part of our work. We invest large amounts of our time, our hearts and money rehabilitating each horse that finds its way to our property. We provide them with the care, medicine, nutrition, training and love that brings them back to a full and productive life. The true magic happens when we help these horses find a new partner a new home, a new chapter.

Whether it was that word, "productive," or the whole mission statement, Carol and I were so taken by it that we were soon on the property, talking to the wonderful, caring volunteers who worked there. As we walked the property with one of the volunteers, I found myself tearing up as I was reminded of the memories I had of my Major over sixty years ago. That, combined with Carol's love of animals and recent interest in horses, cinched it: ERAF would be one of our charities.

Another local charity we discovered was the Big Dog Ranch, located in Loxahatchee Grove, Florida. It was founded in 2008, and since then they have saved the lives of more than fifty thousand dogs. It's a no-kill shelter. Its mission is to rescue, rehabilitate, and educate until every dog has a loving and safe place to call home. As stated on their website, "We believe we can, and we will see and end to dog homelessness and abuse through legislative efforts, hard work and strategic partnerships near and far. We will never give up and we will never back down from the needs of all heartbeats because ever life matters."

Once again, visiting their website revealed a truly state-of-the-art facility encompassing over thirty acres. And once again we were drawn into the wonderful work they do. We were reminded that it's not only some people that need help but also some of our animals that provide us with so much unconditional love, companionship, and loyalty in our lives. We recalled hearing news reports of the Big Dog Ranch making multiple trips by private plane into the Bahamas, rescuing many dogs that were left homeless because of hurricanes hitting the islands in recent times. One can just imagine the chaos and destruction and the vast number of innocent animals left behind in its path. Once again, we made the commitment and added Big Dog Ranch to our list of worthwhile causes to support.

As time goes on and events unfold, it is our plan to combine the assets of our family foundation with those of our family trust to continue the giving after we're gone.

CHAPTER 31

SOME FINAL THOUGHTS

Too often overlooked and seldomly given the attention and importance that it deserves is the effect that a cancer diagnosis has on loved ones, such as the husband or wife who is forced to sit by and watch the effect the disease has on someone they so dearly love. The feelings of helplessness, anger, and frustration are constant. While we try to stay positive every day, inevitably those negative thoughts sneak in and with them a feeling of depression.

Next to the effects of cancer itself, depression is probably the second most destructive side effect. The battle can be lonely and discouraging. It is human nature for the affected person to want to keep those feelings inside because the cancer patient has enough to deal with. But by not talking and keeping those destructive feeling inside, the condition only seems to get worse.

Many choose drugs or alcohol to ease some of the pain. Having spent over thirty years in the beer and alcohol industry, it would be untruthful to say I didn't derive much social pleasure from alcohol. I have always enjoyed a beer after hard labor or while fishing or simply out for a boat ride, or a cocktail or two before dinner with a glass of wine. Over the years I tried hard not to abuse but to rather control that pleasure, although to be honest, there were those times I had too much fun. Never, in the past, however, did I feel I was drinking because I was trying to ease my pain.

Now, not only because I only have one kidney but because of the fear associated with easing the depression and addiction, I try to exert even more control. You constantly ask yourself; Do I have to give up everything I enjoy? For me, the answer is no! I will continue to live my life.

My mom always told me that sometimes when you face difficulty, it is good to count your blessings. As I look back, my life had many blessings and has been pretty cool, if I do say so myself. From my humble childhood beginnings attending a one-room schoolhouse with outdoor plumbing, I met two US presidents, one in office and one after he left office (H. W. Bush and Jerry Ford). I went on an African safari, flew on the Concorde to attend the Royal Ascot horse race in London, went to several Kentucky Derbies and Super Bowls, and partied in the infield of the Indy 500 while also having seats at the first turn on the track. I went to the opening celebration of two US Winter Olympic Games and even traveled on the Orient Express through Scandinavia.

Success is not what you do with it but what you become in the process. I was blessed with wonderful parents and a rewarding career. But, most importantly, God has blessed me with the most wonderful wife, life partner, and soulmate and the love of my life. While it took a while and I wish it would have happened sooner, "I found the one my heart loves" (King James Version, Song of Solomon 3:4), and I pray each day we have many more years together.

It is my hope that if you have cancer and you read my book, you look back at your life the way I have mine. In doing so you will get the mental assurance of hope and appreciation for the life you lived. Success is not what you do with it but what you become in the process. Sometimes I think we take life for granted. In reality it is something God lets us do.

As I traveled this recent journey with all its ups and downs, I learned that when I lost my job at Miller Brewing Company, it was not the end of the world, although at first, I thought it was. The end was not the end at all but simply just the beginning of a new chapter in my life. When our Moscow operation went into bankruptcy, it was not the end, either, and nor were the two years I spent working with the venture capital group trying to consolidate G. Heileman Brewing with the remaining small brewers. And

GUT PUNCH

just like cancer may seem like the end, it doesn't have to be the end either. What I believe now is that for us mortals, the end is not the end at all.

The End

(Or maybe not)

ACKNOWLEDGMENTS

There are several people I would like to acknowledge for their contribution. First is Dr. Eric Hall, who can probably be credited with saving my life by discovering the tumor through his astute observation of a routine ultrasound. I'd also like to thank the following people: My urologist, Dr. David Rodin, and his oncologist wife, Dr. Heather Yeckes-Rodin, who guided me through this overwhelming process and continue to be involved in my journey. Dr. Alice Yu, the young surgeon at Moffitt Cancer center that successfully removed my left kidney, and also at Moffitt, the talented Dr. Jacques-Pierre Fontaine, one of the most respected thoracic surgeons in the country, who successfully removed the melanoma lesions in my lung. Dr. Zeynep Eroglu, also from Moffitt, who was the on-the-scene oncologist and continues to monitor my progress and advise on my local treatment. My dear friend and neighbor Nancy Herold, who recently published her first novel and provided me with valuable feedback and guidance through the process. And finally, my wife and soulmate, Carol, who provided me with the ongoing positive reinforcement and motivation to complete the book writing process as well as the ongoing support through the difficult road to recovery. For all your love and support, I dedicate this book to you.

MEMORIES

THOMAS A KOEHLER

Made in the USA
Columbia, SC
25 November 2024